Man and His Destiny

MAN AND
HIS DESTINY

MURTAZA MUTAHHARI

IBT
Islamic Book Trust
Kuala Lumpur

TOP
Translation of Persian

Published by
Islamic Book Trust
607 Mutiara Majestic
Jalan Othman
46000 Petaling Jaya
Selangor, Malaysia
www.ibtbooks.com

Islamic Book Trust is affiliated with The Other Press Sdn. Bhd.

Perpustakaan Negara Malaysia   Cataloguing-in-Publication Data

Murtaza Mutahhari
    Man and His Destiny / Murtaza Mutahhari.
    ISBN 978-967-0526-50-8
    1. Fate and fatalism--Religious aspects--Islam.
    2. Predestination (Islam).   3. Religious life--Islam.
    I. Title.
    297.22

Printed by
SS Graphic Printers (M) Sdn. Bhd.
Lot 7 & 8, Jalan TIB 3, Taman Industri Bolton,
68100 Batu Caves, Selangor Darul Ehsan.

بِسْمِ ٱللَّهِ مَآ أَصَابَ مِن مُّصِيبَةٍ فِى ٱلْأَرْضِ وَلَا فِىٓ أَنفُسِكُمْ إِلَّا فِى كِتَٰبٍ مِّن قَبْلِ أَن نَّبْرَأَهَآ إِنَّ ذَٰلِكَ عَلَى ٱللَّهِ يَسِيرٌ ۝

"No misfortune can happen on earth or in your souls but is recorded in a decree before We bring it into existence: That is truly easy for Allah."

لِّكَيْلَا تَأْسَوْا۟ عَلَىٰ مَا فَاتَكُمْ وَلَا تَفْرَحُوا۟ بِمَآ ءَاتَىٰكُمْ وَٱللَّهُ لَا يُحِبُّ كُلَّ مُخْتَالٍ فَخُورٍ ۝

"In order that ye may not despair over matters that pass you by, nor exult over favours bestowed upon you. For Allah loveth not any vainglorious boaster."

Sūrah Al-Ḥadīd (The Iron), 57: 22-23

Contents

Short Biography of the Author

Martyr Murtaza Mutahhari was born in Fariman (Iran) in February 1919. His father Shaykh Muhammad Husain was a religious scholar and a pious person. Mutahhari received his elementary education in theology from his father.

When he was twelve years of age, he joined the conventional Islamic School at Mashhad and pursued his studies there for five years. Then he proceeded to Qum, the famous Educational Centre of Shi'ah Muslims. He stayed there for fifteen years and completed his education under the supervision of Allamah Tabatabai, Imam Khumayni and many other distinguished *ulema*.

During the period of his education Prof. Mutahhari felt that the communists wanted to destroy the very spirit of Islam by mixing their atheistic views with the Islamic philosophy and interpreting the verses of the Holy Qur'an in a materialistic manner. Of course, communism was misguiding the young generation, which prompted the professor to nip this threat in the bud.

He wrote extensively against the baneful effects of communism.

He also wrote on exegesis, philosophy, ethics, sociology, history and many other subjects. He left over twenty books that have been published in Persian, Arabic, Turkish, Urdu and English. The Islamic Seminary has had the honour of publishing some of them.

In 1952, he established a council of university students in Tehran and, in 1955, began teaching theology at the University of Tehran at the doctorate level continuing until 1978. He remained faithful to his socio-political commitments. In 1963, he was arrested along with Imam Khumayni. After the exile of Imam Khumayni to Turkey, he took active part in the leadership of the Islamic movement, making decisive contributions to the mobilization of the combatant *ulema*.

After the success of Islamic Revolution in Iran he was nominated as the President of the Constitutional Council and was performing his duties in a very befitting manner. The activities of this scholar were intolerable for the followers of the atheistic schools and they, therefore, decided to remove him from the scene by terroristic methods. Eventually they assassinated this eminent scholar on May 1, 1979. His martyrdom was a great tragedy. When the sad news was conveyed to Imam Khumayni he could not control his tears. In his condolence message he said:

"In him I have lost a dear son. I am mourning the death of one who was the fruition of my life."

Thousands and thousands of Muslims escorted his funeral. He was laid to rest in Qum in the precincts of the Holy Shrine of Ma'suma in Qum. May his soul rest in peace.

Prologue

The question of fate and destiny that forms the subject matter of this book is a philosophical question, and should normally be looked for in the books of philosophy. But here in this book it has been taken out of its proper context and placed along with some other questions.

All scientific and philosophical questions are classed in accordance with the subject with which they deal or the purpose for which they are studied.

The reason why the philosophical questions form one class, the mathematical another and the physical a third, is that there is a special common link between the questions dealt with by each set of these questions or at least there exists some common theoretical or practical objects which may be achieved by its study.

The question of destiny and fate is classed as a philosophical question. But in this book it has grouped with the questions with which it is connected neither with regard to its subject nor with regard to the object of its study.

Here this question is being studied under the heading of "The causes of the decline of the Muslims". This heading includes multifarious subjects, events and questions, some of them being historical, others psychological, moral, social or purely religious. A few of them are philosophical also. Thus a large number of subjects belonging to various classes and categories form a part of this study.

The only link which binds these subjects together is their positive or negative effects on the progress and the decline of the Muslim society.

The aim of raising this question in this book is to see whether a belief in destiny as required by philosophical reasoning is one of those ideas which lead their adherents to lethargy and lack of vigor. Are the people who believe in it automatically dragged to decline and decay or is it a doctrine which has no bad effect provided it is expounded in a sound manner. It is also to see how Islam has presented this question and with what effect on its followers. This being the only aim of those aspects of the question which have no bearing on it, have been left out.

I do not remember exactly since when I have been interested in the question of the causes of the decline of the Muslims and have been thinking about it. But it may be claimed with certainty that for the past few years, this question has been engaging my attention. During this period I have either myself been thinking over it or reading what others have written. Whenever I came across a writing on this subject, I read it with interest and tried to comprehend the view-point of the writer. This was my practice till one day while I was talking about an authentic *hadīth* accepted by both the Shi'ah and Sunnis, to the effect that: "Islam is to have an upper hand; it is not to be suppressed".

I realized that what I had read or heard till then, though

useful, was not convincing. As I found that like me my listeners were also deeply interested in the subject, I decided to study it more thoroughly and minutely. I felt that any improvement in the present position of the Muslim world largely depended on ascertaining the causes of its decline. For this purpose it was necessary not only to study as far as possible the views of others, both Muslims and non-Muslims, but to make a comprehensive study of all the relevant subjects including those which have not so far been studied from this angle.

It was here that I was struck by the vast magnitude of the problem. I realized that it was not possible for one individual to make a scientific inquiry into all the relevant subjects. This job at least required many long years. Anyhow I decided to do the preliminary work and then to study one or two subjects in detail as a test case. If some other people apply themselves to other subjects, it is hoped that a useful study of an important social subject will be completed with a sort of joint effort and mutual co-operation.

There is no doubt that the Muslims have left behind the most brilliant period of their history. At one time they were not only the rulers of the world, but, what is more important, were the standard-bearers of human culture. The world has witnessed many rulers and conquerors who imposed their will on others for some time, but before long they were wiped out like froth of water. That was not the case with the Muslims. They brought about an unparalleled intellectual awakening and founded a brilliant culture which lasted for several centuries. It is still celebrated as a golden link of the chain of human culture, and history itself is proud of the illustrious achievement of the Muslims. For so many centuries the Muslims excelled in sciences, crafts, philosophy, art, morals and higher social order throughout the world. Others have borrowed much from them. Many unbiased investigators have admitted that the wonderful civilization of modern Europe which today runs supreme in the whole world was inspired by the magnificent Islamic culture.

Gustave Le Bon says:

"Some Europeans feel shy to admit that a heathen nation is responsible for their emergence from barbarism and ignorance, and for that reason they conceal this fact. But their unreasonable attitude is extremely regrettable ... It was the moral influence of the Muslim Arabs that humanized the European people who had toppled the Roman Empire. It opened the door of sciences, arts and philosophy to those who were totally ignorant of such things. These Arabs were for 600 years the teachers of us, the Europeans".

Will Durant in his *History of Civilization* says:

"The inception and decline of Islamic culture has been a big historical event. During the five centuries from 81 A.H. to 594 A.H. Islam was the world champion in regards to military power, law and order, good morals, developed life, human and just laws, religious tolerance, literature, scientific investigation, medicine and philosophy."

He further says:

"The Muslim world exercised its influence on the Christian world in various ways. From Muslim countries, Europe imported food, syrups, medicines, weapons, tools, artistic taste, industrial and commercial methods, laws and maritime practices. It also borrowed from the Muslim languages. The

Arab (Muslim) scholars learnt Greek, mathematics, physics, chemistry, astronomy and medicine. They further developed them and conveyed the Greek heritage in a richer form to Europe. The Arab (Muslim) physicians preserved the works of Aristotle for Christian Europe and incidentally altered them. From among the oriental philosophers Avicenna (Ibn Sina) and Averroes (Ibn Rushd) influenced the European philosophers. Their skill was as reliable as that of the Greeks ... This Muslim influence penetrated to Europe through trade, the crusades, the translation of thousands of books from Arabic to Latin and the travelling of the European scholars to Andalus."

He also says:

"Only during golden epochs of history a society is able to produce in a short time all such luminaries in the field of politics, education, literature, language, geography, history, mathematics, astronomy, chemistry, philosophy, medicine etc. as were produced by Islam during the four centuries from the time of Harun al-Rashid to that of Averroes. A part of the brilliant activities of the Muslim was based on the works of the Greeks, but a major portion of them especially in the fields of politics, poetry and art was strikingly original".

It was an admitted fact that the illustrious phenomenon known as 'Islamic culture' continued to exist for centuries before it vanished. Today the Muslims as compared to many other nations and to their own glorious past are in a pitiable state of decline and backwardness.

Naturally a question arises as to why the Muslims have retrograded after making all these achievements in sciences, arts, crafts and organizational matters. What is the cause of their decline and retrogression and who is responsible for their present pitiable state? Is it the fault of certain individuals or groups? Or was it because of certain events that the Muslims deviated from their original course? Is it natural that every nation makes progress during a limited period and then as a matter of course its decline begins?

If it is admitted that some particular factor has been responsible for the decline of the Muslims, we must identify that factor. Some Europeans (not all) who are biased because of their Christian prejudice or their imperialistic propensities blame Islam itself for the backwardness of the Muslims. Are they right? Or is it that instead of Islam, the Muslims are to be blamed? Or is it that the fault lies with those non-Muslim nations which have in various ways come in contact with Muslims during the past fourteen centuries? The answer to these questions is not a simple affair. It requires a comparatively lengthy discussion. Every alternative is to be weighed and investigated scientifically. Before entering into this discussion, the following preliminary points are naturally to be considered:

- The extent of the glory and splendour and Islamic culture.

- The causes that led to the flourishing of Islamic culture.

- Islam's contribution to the progress of the Muslims.

- Contribution of the Islamic culture to the modern European culture.

- The present position of the Muslim world as indicated by the signs of its backwardness.

- Though Islamic culture has disappeared, Islam is still a

living, active and expanding force, and rivals the most powerful new social and revolutionary forces.

▪ Muslim people are awakening and are trying to stand on their own feet again.

After completing this preliminary discussion which requires a separate book, it is necessary to undertake a deep philosophical discussion of the nature of time to ascertain whether it is true, as claimed by some philosophers of history, that what causes the progress and advancement of a nation, causes its decline also. In other words, every factor can only under certain conditions related to a particular period, push forward a society, and with a change in the circumstances and with the beginning of a new era of history, it loses its vitality and ceases to be a pushing force. Then it automatically becomes the cause of its decline.

Should this philosophy be true, every culture should disappear because of the same factors which contributed to its promotion. There is no need of the introduction of any foreign factor. All old factors are, to say, reactionary, and new factors progressive. New social factors give rise to a new culture which by its very nature is different from the old one. Should this rule be true, naturally the Islamic culture cannot be an exception to it. In that case it is useless to discuss the cause of the decline of the Muslims, for they cannot be discussed independently and in isolation from the factors which gave rise to Muslim culture. According to this philosophy it is not necessary to hold any person, group or event responsible for the decline of the Muslims. Islamic culture disappeared, because every culture has to disappear one day. Every living phenomenon has sooner or later to die its natural or unnatural death. Islamic culture too was born. It grew. It matured. It superannuated and then died. To wish for its revival is tantamount to wishing for the revival of the dead; which is not natural and can be effected only by some miraculous cause, the bringing about of which is after all beyond human control.

After a preliminary study of the various aspects of the glory and decline of the Muslims we come to this important philosophical-historical question which cannot be overlooked, for in this connection there was already been much worthless talk, and many people have been influenced by immature views.

The philosophical study of this question will be incomplete unless the question of the conformity of Islam to the requirements of the time is also thoroughly investigated. This discussion will naturally consist of two parts: the first part will be purely philosophical and the second one Islamic. Both the parts are worth consideration under one heading, 'Islam and the requirements of time'.

When I finished this study I came to the conclusion that the above mentioned philosophical rule was untenable. I could not believe that the causes of the decline of the Muslims were necessarily the same as those of their progress. Now the time has come that we should study the causes of the stagnation, decline and backwardness of the Muslims and see what others have said in this connection.

Considering what others, both Muslims and non-Muslims, have said and keeping in view the questions and the events which are naturally to be considered in this connection, this study will have to be undertaken in three sections:

- Section of Islam.

- Section of Muslims.

- Section of Foreign factors.

Each section consists of a number of subjects and questions. For example, someone may hold the Islamic tenets to be responsible for the decline of the Muslims. Some others may think that the moral system of Islam producers degenerating effect. Still some others may maintain that the social laws of Islam are the real causes of the decline of the Muslims. Incidentally, this charge has actually been leveled against certain doctrines, moral principles and social laws of Islam.

Similarly in the other two sections also there are many questions which are to be considered.

In this connection, the following Islamic tenets and doctrines have to be especially considered:

- Belief in fate and destiny.

- Belief in the hereafter and the disparagement of this worldly life.

- Intercession.

- Dissimulation.

- Expectation of solace (the advent of Mahdi the Occult Imam).

Out of these five doctrines the first three are common between the Shi‘ah and sunni.

Sometimes it is said that the real cause of the decline of the Muslims is their belief in fate and destiny. And sometimes it is said that the importance which Islam attaches to the next world and its everlasting life has diverted the attention of the Muslims from the problems of life. Again some people say that the belief in intercession, which has existed during all periods of Islamic history and which has been upheld by all Muslims except a few, has made the Muslims indifferent to the sins. The only deterrent against the sins is the fear of their evil consequences. As the Muslims hope for intercession, they feel no need to abstain from any vice or crime.

The two doctrines peculiar to the Shi'ah, the dissimulation and the expectation of solace are also criticized in this connection. It is said that the doctrine of dissimulation in the first place means hypocrisy and double-facedness, and in the second it has rendered the Shi'ah timid, weak and unable to face the facts of life boldly. In connection with the expectation of solace[1] it is said that this doctrine has deprived the Shi'ah of every initiative to improve their condition. While all other nations of the world are making efforts to improve their lot, the Shi'ah are waiting for the appearance of a saviour.

Out of the Islamic moral principles, austerity, contentment, patience, satisfaction, submission to the will of Allah and trust in Him have been charged with having a hand in the decadence of the Muslims.

Out of the administrative rules of Islam which fall in this category, the most important is the question of government. According to some critics Islam has failed to determine the duties of the Muslims clearly in this respect.

The penal laws of Islam have since long been ignored by the Muslims, and the Muslim countries have replaced them with the alien laws, though with unfortunate results. Nevertheless the penal laws of Islam are still begin criticized.

---

[1] See, *The Awaited Saviour*, ISP 1979.

Two provisions of the Islamic civil law have been especially criticized during the modern times. One of them is the question of the rights of women and the other that of the economic laws of Islam in respect of property and inheritance.

Many people feel upset by the restrictions imposed by Islam on the relations between the Muslims and the non-Muslims, such as the rules in respect of marriage between a Muslim and a non-Muslim, meat of the animal slaughtered by a non-Muslim and the uncleanliness of the infidels as described in Islamic jurisprudence. These questions are regarded as the factors contributing to the backwardness of the Muslims.

These are the subjects in the section of Islam which need investigation and thorough study.

Fortunately favorable conditions for such an investigation exist now and it is possible to clarify these questions and remove any doubts about them lurking in the mind of the young and the educated classes.

Next section is that of the Muslims. In this section our attention is concentrated on the Muslims instead of Islam. In other words, we ascertain if it is true, that it is the Muslims themselves who are responsible for their decadence by deviating from the teachings of Islam.

In this section also we face many questions. First of all we have to determine what are the points of deviation and to find out what teachings of Islam have been abandoned by the Muslims and which practices foreign to Islam have been adopted by them. Secondly, we have to see whether the Muslims generally are responsible for their decadence or only leading sections of them.

It is known that Islam first appeared among the Arabs and

thereafter spread to other nations such as the Iranians, the Indians, the Copts, the Berbers *etc.* All these people had their own national, racial and historic characteristics. It is to be seen whether these people or some of them influenced Islam through their characteristics and diverted it from its original course in such a way that if it had gone to some other nations, for example the Europeans, the destiny of Islamism and the Muslims would have been different today. Or is it that the Muslim masses had no role in this respect and whatever damage has been done to Islam and the Muslims, was wrought by the two influential classes, namely, the rulers and the divines.

In the section of foreign factors there are many events which must attract attention. From the very beginning Islam has always faced the hostility of its internal and external enemies. The Jews, the Christians, the Zoroastrians, the Manicheans and the heretics among the Muslims themselves, were not idle. They stabbed Islam in the back whenever they got an opportunity. Many of them played an active role in distorting the Islamic facts by fabricating *ḥadīths* (traditions) or by creating new sects and sowing the seeds of dissention. If they could do nothing else, they fanned the differences among the Muslims.

In Islamic history we come across many political or religious movements started by the non-Muslims with a view to weakening or obliterating Islam.

Occasionally the Muslim world was subjected to a large scale invasion also. The crusades and the Mongol invasion are the outstanding examples.

The western imperialism did even more harm during the past few centuries. It sucked the blood of the Muslims and sapped their energy under the pressure of its oppressive policies.

Imam Khumayni, the leader of the oppressed nations of the world has said:

"The Muslims of the world should make a united effort to regain the lost glory of Islam. It should be clearly remembered by one and all that those who spur up disunity among the ranks of the Muslims are neither Sunnis nor Shi'ahs; they are lackeys of the imperialists whose only aim is to destroy Islam."

In view of what has been stated above, the subjects which should be considered are the following:

Spectacular progress of the Muslims and their decline (This subject is preliminary to the rest of the study);

Islam and the requirements of time (This subject has two parts: the first is related to the philosophy of history and the second deals with the application of the Islamic rules in the changing circumstances. This study also has a preliminary aspect).

Fate and destiny

- Belief in the hereafter and its effect on the progress and decline.
- Intercession.
- Dissimulation.
- Expectation of solace.
- Moral system of Islam.
- Islamic view about the government.
- Islamic economy.

- Penal laws of Islam.
- Rights of woman in Islam.
- International law of Islam.
- Points of deviation.
- Forgery and fabrication of *hadīths*.
- Shi'ah-Sunni differences and their contribution to the decline of the Muslims.
- Ash'arism and Mu'tazilism.
- Stagnation and *ijtihad*.
- Philosophy and mysticism (*irfan*).
- Rulers of the Muslim world.
- Leadership of *ulema*.
- Subversive activities of the minorities in the Muslim world.
- Crusades.
- Fall of Andalus.
- Mongol invasion.
- Imperialism.

These are the subjects which in my view should be included in this study. I do not claim to be exhaustive or to have been able to arrange them in an ideal order. There may possibly be some other subjects which should have been included in this list but have been missed by me. I know that I have neither capacity nor time to deal with all these subjects alone, but in some of them, including No. 1 and 2, I have prepared notes and hope to be able to publish them as early as possible.

I shall be highly obliged if some other writers and eminent

scholars could choose a subject of their liking, carry out necessary investigations.

Some twenty years back when I first noticed that the Europeans regard the belief in fate and destiny as a cause or even the main cause of the decadence of the Muslims, I was still a student at the Islamic Educational Centre at Qum.

I was reading the second volume of *The Life of Muḥammad* by Muhammad Husayn Haykal. The final portion of the book consisted of two articles.

- Islamic culture as explained by the Qur'an.

- Orientalists and Islamic culture.

In the course of the second article he has reproduced what the well-known American writer, Washington Irving has said in his book about the Holy Prophet (ṣ). According to Haykal, towards the end of his book after explaining the Islamic tenets about faith in Allah, the Angels, the Scriptures, the Prophets and the Day of Resurrection, Washington Irving said:

"The last and the sixth fundamental principle of Islam is that of predestination. Muḥammad used it for the advancement of his warfare, for according to his rule every event which occurs in the world is already predetermined in the knowledge of God and is recorded in the 'protected tablet'. The destiny of everybody and the time of his death are predetermined and unalterable. Nothing can advance or delay an event. The Muslims who believed in these points and regarded them as indisputable, attacked the enemy fearlessly during a battle. They looked upon death during a fighting to be equal to martyrdom, which ensured Paradise. That is why they were sure of victory in either case, whether they were killed or overpowered the enemy.

Of course, there are some Muslims who consider the theory of predestination, which says that man is not free to avoid sins, to be contrary to the justice and mercy of God. Certain sects have emerged which have tried and are still trying to explain and modify the doctrine of predestination, but their number is small and they are not considered to be the followers of the practice of the Prophet ... There could be no doctrine better than that which could drive the uninformed and self-conceited soldiers to the battlefield, and assure them of spoils if they survived and of Paradise if they were killed. This belief made the Muslim soldiers so bold and mighty that no other soldiers could rival them. But still this belief was a poison which annihilated the influence of Islam in the long run. When the successors of the Prophet gave up the policy of fighting wars and making conquests, and sheathed their swords, the doctrine of predestination revealed its devastating characteristics. Peace and tranquility weakened the nerves of the Muslims.

The material comforts allowed by Islam, which distinguish this religion from Christianity, a religion of purity and self-negation, also had their effect. The Muslims ascribed all their sufferings and hardships to fate and regarded it as their duty to bear them patiently. According to them and any human effort and knowledge was of no avail in getting rid of them. The followers of Muhammad gave no importance to the golden rule: 'God helps those who help themselves'. That is why the Cross replaced the Crescent. If the Crescent still has some influence in Europe, that is because the big Christian powers want that to be so. In other words the influence of the Crescent is due to the mutual of its influence is a fresh proof of the maxim that anything gained by the power of sword, is taken away by the power of sword only."

Haykal in reply to this American has given a detailed explanation according to his own thinking and taste. His explanation, though it contains many good points, is not methodical, and hence it is controversial and can be refuted.

In this book we propose to prove the baselessness of the statement of Washington Irving and other Europeans and show that the doctrine of fate and destiny is miles apart from the theory of predestination. We will show that the same soldiers of early Islam, whom Mr. Washington Irving arrogantly describes as uninformed and self-conceited, were fully aware of the difference which he is unable to comprehend.

Secondly, the Qur'an itself has supported human liberty in a number of its verses. Those who advocated the doctrine of free will and described the theory of predestination as opposed to the justice and mercy of Allah (*viz.* The Shi'ah and the Mu'tazilites), contrary to the assertion of the orientalists, did not go against the teachings of the Qur'an, nor did they modify what the Qur'an had said. Actually they derived their view from the Qur'an itself.

Thirdly, this great writer who, according to Haykal is a biased Christian and who calls Christianity a religion of purity and self-negation because unlike Islam it has given no heed to the problems of life, refers to the eternal Divine knowledge sarcastically. Is it possible that a person believing in God may deny His eternal knowledge of everything? Is it a fault of the Qur'an that it describes Allah as All-Knowing?

Fourthly, he says that the followers of Muḥammad (ṣ) did not give importance to the rule that 'God helps those who help themselves'.

This writer did not take the trouble of reading a translation of the Holy Qur'an even once, otherwise he would not have made such a frivolous assertion. The Qur'an expressly says:

"As for him who desires the hereafter, strives for it as he should, and is a true believer, it is such people whose efforts shall be appreciated by Allah. We help both these and those with the favour of your Lord and more is deprived of it (in this world)".

Sūrah Al-Isrā', 17:19-20

The followers of Muhammad attained even a higher stage of self-reliance, when they believed in the teaching of the Qur'an saying:

"If you help Allah, He will help you and will make your foothold firm".

Sūrah Muḥammad, 47:7

The Qur'an did not say: *"If you help yourselves ..."* because that expression would have smacked of cupidity and personal profit. Instead it has used the expression: *"If you help Allah"*, which has a general and human aspect and implies service to humanity. As for the ascendancy of the Cross over the Crescent, which is regarded by Washington Irving as final and everlasting, we will discuss this point later at a suitable place in this book.

These views are not peculiar to Mr. Washington Irving. Similar views have been expressed by almost all other European writers, including those who appear to be unbiased to a certain extent. They all agree that Islam is a pre-destinarian creed. The only difference is that some of them do not regard this as a factor responsible for the decadence of the Muslims, whereas some others maintain that it is. Some European authors have even declared it to be main cause of the decline of the Muslims.

Will Durant in his *History of Civilization* after referring to the Qur'anic verses regarding the omnipotence and knowledge of Allah says:

> Predestinarianism is an essential part of Islamic thinking. In consequence of this belief the faithful endured the severest hardships of life with equanimity. But during the last few centuries it has blocked the progress of the Arabs and numbed their thinking power.

In contrast, Gustave Le Bon maintains that the belief in predestination was not a cause of the decline of the Muslims, and that the causes of their decline should be looked for somewhere else.

At first I intended to mention all the points connected with the progress and the decline of the Muslims in the introduction prefixed to this book. But later I gave up the idea, for if the necessary details of all the points were given, the introduction would have become lengthier than the main book and if brevity was observed that would not have served the purpose. Hence I preferred to be contented with what has been mentioned as an illustration. The details may be given in a separate treatise.

In this book, not all the points and the questions related to fate and destiny have been mentioned, because the aim is only to study whether this doctrine has actually been a cause of the decline of the Muslims. Hence certain aspects of this question which appeared to be irrelevant for our present purpose, have been omitted.

The question of fate has a long history among the Muslims.

The expounders of the Qur'an, the scholastic theologians, the philosophers, the mystics, and even the poets and the literary figures have all discussed this question. An account of the views expressed by them requires an independent book. Besides, this question is covered by a large number of the Qur'anic verses and the *ḥadīths* (traditions) which are a model of the depth of Islamic knowledge. These very verses and *ḥadīths* have guided the Muslim philosophers and have enriched the Islamic philosophy to the extent pre-Islamic Greek philosophy paled in comparison to it.

Furthermore, there exist some other connected questions in the Islamic teachings that are not easy to explain by means of logical reasoning. One such point is *Laylah al-Qadr* (The Night of Destiny) which has been expressly mentioned in the Holy Qur'an, and about which there is no difference of opinion between the Shi'ah and the Sunnis. Another point is that of *Bada'* (Divine exposition), which is an indisputable Shi'ah doctrine based on the Qur'anic text.[2] Predestination, free will and human liberty are the questions which if considered from various psychological, moral, philosophical and social angles, will require too lengthy a discussion.

It is hoped this book will prove useful and interesting to the inquisitive reader, and it would also remove his doubts in regard to the subject discussed, and would enlighten him to an appreciable degree.

---

[2] See, *The Beliefs of the Shi'ite School*, Islamic Seminary Publications, 1985.

CHAPTER 1

Fate and Destiny are the Words that Cause Alarm

No two words more awful than fate and destiny have ever struck the ears of a human being.

Nothing can be more depressing to the spirit of a man than the feeling that he has no liberty and all his acts are controlled by a superpower.

It may be said that freedom and liberty are the supreme blessings and the most bitter disappointment is supreme blessing and the most bitter disappointment is a feeling of helplessness, a feeling that one has no independent personality, a feeling that he is just like a sheep in the hands of a shepherd and that he has no control even over his food, sleep, life and death.

A feeling of quiet endurance and resignation resulting from helplessness is more consuming and oppressive to human spirit than any king of fire.

That is the position when a man finds himself helpless against another who is more powerful or against an animal which is stronger. It is easy to imagine what his position will be if he finds himself dominated by an invisible and mysterious force which he cannot resist. Obviously his position will be far worse.

A question which has always engaged human attention is whether the affairs of this world are going on in accordance with a pre-arranged and inevitable program. Are all the events in this world governed by an invisible but immensely powerful force called fate and destiny? Is everything that is happening now or will ever happen, predetermined? Is man subject to determinism and has no liberty of choosing? Or is it that there is no such thing as fate and man is absolutely free to determine his own destiny? Or is it that actually there operates a third alternative, according to which all events of the world are governed by destiny, the influence of which extends to everything without exception, but still its irresistible influence does not curtail human liberty in the least. If this is the case, how is it to be explained?

The question of fate and destiny is one of the most equivocal philosophical questions. For certain reasons to be explained later, it has been a subject of dispute among the Muslim thinkers from the first century of the Hijri era. The various views held in this connection have caused many controversies and given rise to a number of sects in the Muslim world with queer results during the past fourteen centuries.

Though it is a so called metaphysical subject, for two reasons it also comes under the category of practical and social questions.

The first reason is that man's way of thinking about this question affects his practical life and social attitude.

It is obvious that the spirit and attitude of a man looking at himself as a being subject to inexorable determinism, is different from those of one who believes that he has been created free and hence he is master of his destiny.

Generally speaking, most of the philosophical questions do not affect the spirit, attitude and actions of man. The practical attitude and the social spirit of a person are not influenced by such questions as the temporal eternity or transcience of the universe, the finiteness or infinitude of its dimensions, the system of causation, the theory that many cannot emanate from one and the identicalness of the essence and the attributes of the Self-existent Being.

The second reason is that the doctrine of fate and destiny, despite its being a personal belief, comes under the category of the questions of universal application, for the number of people who are in search of its solutions is very large.

It is one of those questions which engage the attention of nearly all those who have some capacity of thinking over general questions. Everybody is naturally interested in knowing whether he is at liberty to determine his course of life or it has already been irrevocably determined by his fate.

The scope of other philosophical questions is limited. They are only a matter of personal and private interest and do not attract such a general attention.

From these two view-points this question may be included in the category of practical, universal and social problems.

In olden days attention was seldom paid to the practical and social effects of this question. It was discussed only from theoretical, philosophical and scholastic points of view. But modern scholars give more heed to its practical and social aspects, and look at it from the angle of its effect on the way of thinking of the nations and their progress and decline.

Some critics of Islam hold that the biggest cause of the decline of the Muslims is their faith in fate and destiny. Now a question arises, if belief in destiny is a cause of the decline of an individual or a society, how is it that the early Muslims were not adversely affected by it. Did they not have a belief in destiny? Was this question introduced in the teachings of Islam later, as asserted by some European historians? Or is it that the nature of their belief in fate and destiny was such that it was not inconsistent with their faith in liberty and responsibility? In other worlds, did they believe that one's destiny was not absolutely beyond his control and that he could change it. If so, what was the basis of their thinking?

Leaving aside the basis of their belief, let us see what the Qur'an and the Imams say in this respect. Then we will see what way of thinking we should logically adopt.

Verses of The Qur'an

Some verses of the Holy Qur'an expressly support the rule of destiny. They state that nothing happens in the world without the Will of Allah and that every event is already recorded in the 'Book'.

A few of the Qur'anic verses to this effect are quoted:

"Every affliction that falls on the earth or yourselves, already exists in a Book before it is brought into being by us. No doubt that is easy for Allah to accomplish".

Sūrah Al-Ḥadīd, 57:22

"With Him are the keys of the invisible. None but He knows them. And He knows what is in the land and the sea. Not a leaf

falls, but he knows it, not a grain amid the darkness of the earth, nor anything green or withered but is recorded in a clear Book".

Sūrah Al-Anʿām, 6:59

It is often seen that in the sentence, *"there is nothing green or withered, but it is recorded in a clear Book"*, the word, Book is taken to be referring to the Qur'an, but it may be said with certainly that here the word, 'Book' does not refer to it. So far as we know, not a single reliable expounder of the Qur'an has interpreted the verse that way.

"They said: Do we have any say in the matter? Muhammad, tell them: All matters belong to Allah. They try to bide within themselves what they do not reveal to you, saying: Had we had the matter in our hands, we would not have been slain there. Say: Even though you had been in your houses, those appointed to be slain would have been slain by your sworn enemies while you were in your beds".

Sūrah Āl ʿImrān, 3:154

"We hold the store of everything and we send it down in an appointed measure".

Sūrah Al-Ḥijr, 15:21

"Allah has set a measure for all things".

Sūrah Al-Talāq, 65:2

"Surely We created everything by measure".

Sūrah Al-Qamar, 54:49

"Then it is for Allah to have in error whom He will and to guide whom He pleases. He is the Mighty, the Wise".

Sūrah Ibrāhīm, 14:4

"Say: Allah! Owner of Sovereignty! You bestow sovereignty on whomever you will and you withdraw from whomever you will. In your Hand is all that is good. No doubt you have power to do everything".

Sūrah Āl ʿImrān, 3:26

There are other verses which indicate that man is free and he can change his destiny:

"Allah never changes the condition of a nation unless it change what is in its heart".

Sūrah Al-Raʿd, 13:11

"Allah coins a similitude: a town whose people that lived secure and well content. Its provisions came in abundance from every quarter, but its people denied the favours of Allah, so He afflicted them with famine and fear because of what they used to do".

Sūrah Al-Naḥl, 16:112

"Allah did not do injustice to them, but they had wronged themselves".

Sūrah Al-ʿAnkabūt, 29:40

"Your Lord does no injustice to His slaves".

Sūrah Fuṣṣilat, 41:46

"We have shown man the right path. Now it is upto him to be grateful or thankless".

Sūrah Al-Dahr, 76:3

"Muḥammad say: This is the truth from your Lord. Let him who believe in it, and let him who will reject it".

Sūrah Al-Kahf, 18:29

"Corruption has become rife on land and sea because of the misdeeds of the people".

Sūrah Al-Rūm, 30:41

"Whoever seeks the harvest of the hereafter, We shall give it to him in abundance, and whoever seeks the harvest of the world, We give him a share of it. But in the hereafter he shall have no share".

Sūrah Al-Shūrā, 42:20

"As for him who desires the worldly pleasures, We swiftly provide in this world whatever We will to whomever We please. Then we assign to him Hell in which he shall burn despised and rejected. As for him who desires the hereafter, strives for it as he should, and is a true believer, it is such people whose efforts shall be appreciated by Allah. Each group will receive its share from the bounty of your Lord. And the bounty of your Lord is not limited"

Sūrah Al-Isrā', 17:18-20

There are many other verses of both the categories. Most of the expounders of the Qur'an and the scholastic theologians consider the verses of the two categories to be contradictory to each other. According to them it is necessary to accept the verses of one category and explain away those of the other. This way of thinking appeared in the second half of the first century. The exponents of human liberty and the doctrine of free will tried to interpret the verses of the first category. They came to be known as the Qadarites. Another group inclined to the doctrine of predestination, interpreted the verses of the second category, and was called the Jabarite or predestinarian. Gradually two big groups of the scholastic theologians, two schools of theology came to be recognized. They absorbed in their ranks both the Jabarites and the Qadarites which ceased to exist independently. The Ash'arite school advocated predestination and the Mu'tazailite supported doctrine of free will.

Qadarite

We have used the word Qadarite for the advocates of human liberty and free will. This term has been used in this sense by most of the scholastic theologians. In the religious reports also this word mostly has the same meaning. Anyhow, occasionally this term has been applied to the Jabarites also. On the whole, both the exponents of free will and predestination did not like themselves to be called the Qadarites, and applied this term to their opponents. The reason of this abhorrence was that a *ḥadīth* was current according to which the Holy Prophet (ṣ) was reported to have said that the 'Qadarites were the Magians of the Muslim *ummah* (nation)'. The Jabarites said that the term, 'Qadarites' referred to those who denied *taqdir* (destiny). Their opponents held that the Qadarites were those who believed that everything, including human acts, was predestined. Anyhow, for two reasons this term stuck to those who denied destiny: Firstly because the Ash'arite school became popular and the number of its opponents went on decreasing and secondly because the Qadarites were compared to the Magians, who were known to be confirming Divine destiny to what they called 'good'. Evil was ascribed by them to *Ahriman* (Devil).

Conflicting Views

We have already said that according to the most of the interpreters of the Qur'an as well as the scholastic theologians, the Qur'anic verses in respect of destiny and human free will are conflicting and hence it was necessary that the verses of one of these two categories should be interpreted in a way different from what they apparently convey. It may be mentioned here that there are two kinds of contradiction. Sometimes a statement expressly contradicts another. For example, someone says: "The Holy Prophet died in the month of Safar". Another person says. "The Prophet did not die in the month of Safar". In this case the second statement expressly repudiates the first. But sometimes the position is somewhat different. The second statement does not contradict the first, but the truth of the second implies its falsity. For example, someone says: "The Prophet died in the month of Rabial-Awwal". It is self-evident that if the Prophet died in the month of Rabi'al-Awwal, he could not have died in the month of Safar.

Now let us see how the verses of the Qur'an in regard to fate and destiny on the one hand, and human liberty and free will on the other are mutually incompatible. Are they of the first type and expressly contradict each other, or of the second and the import of the verses of one category denies that of the verses of the other category.

There is no doubt that the Qur'anic verses on this subject do not expressly contradict each other. The position is not that the verses of one category say that everything is destined and those of the second declare that there is no such thing as destiny; or that the verses of one category say that man is free and has a choosing power, but those of the second category assert that man is not free and has no choice. No verses of the Qur'an deny that the Knowledge of Allah is all-comprehensive and that everything depends on His Will. The reason why the two sets of these verses are considered to be conflicting is that the scholastic theologians and some commentators of the Qur'an think that destiny implies that man is not free. According to them destiny and liberty are mutually inconsistent. They argue that the fact that everything is within the Knowledge of Allah means that everything has been predetermined by Him. Should it be admitted that man exercise his own free will, Allah's Knowledge may on many occasions prove wrong.

In contrast, if it is true that man is master of his destiny and an effective factor in making or marring his fortune that automatically means that nothing is predestined.

Hence, one out of these two sets of verses needs interpretation.

The commentaries of the Holy Qur'an and the scholastic books of the Ash'arites and the Mu'tazilites are full of explanations and interpretations on this point. The Mu'tazilites explain the verses referring to destiny and the Ash'arites interpret those related to free will. To see the specimens of these interpretations a reference may be made to *Tafsir al-Kashshaf* by Zamakhshari, whose way of thinking is that of the Mu'tazilites.

Now let us see if it is feasible to have a third view which may resolve the apparent conflict between the belief in fate and destiny on the one hand and Allah's Omnipotence and His Omniscience on the other. If we can find such a proposition there will be no need of interpreting any set of the Qur'anic verses.

As we will see later there already exists a third view, according to which there is no actual conflict between these two sets of the Qur'anic verses. As a matter of fact, conflict has been created by a misunderstanding on the part of some theologians and commentators. On principle it is meaningless to say that there is any contradiction in the Qur'an and that it is necessary to reconcile the conflicting verses. The fact is that there is not a single verse which may require any reconciliation. That is not the case even with the so called most equivocal verses. The consistency of the Qur'an is a subject which requires detailed discussion, but it is beyond the scope of this book. Anyhow, it may be said safely that constancy is one of the most miraculous aspects of the Holy Book.

CHAPTER 2

Evil Effects of the
Doctrine of Predestination

There is no doubt that the doctrine of predestination, as enunciated by the Ash'arites, who maintain that man absolutely lacks liberty and freedom is dangerous. It paralyses the spirit and will of man. This doctrine encourages the oppressors and binds the hands of the credulous oppressed. Those who are able to occupy wrongly a position which they do not deserve or acquire wealth by unlawful mean, always talk of the blessing and favour of Allah.

They say that He favours whomsoever he likes. His bounty is endless. That is the plea advanced by them to justify their unlawful gains. The under-privileged do not dare to make any protest, because they think that their protest would amount to raising objection against what Allah has ordained. Hence they endure their lot patiently. This doctrine provides the unjust an easy pretext of absolving himself of the responsibility of his misdeeds. The persecuted believes that whatever befalls him, is directed from Allah and therefore to fight against any act of injustice and tyranny is not only absurd but is also immoral.

A believer in predestination does not care to promote his personality, to reform his moral conduct and to control his actions because he disbelieves in the system of cause and effect and gives no heed to the relationship between man, his deeds and his spiritual and moral personality on the one hand and his happy or miserable future on the other. He leaves everything to his fate.

Political Misuse

History show that during the Umayyad period the rulers made full use of the doctrine of fate and destiny. They were staunch supporters of predestination, and persecuted those who preached self-respect, liberty and free will. That is why this sentence became proverbial: Predestinarianism and anthropomorphism are the doctrines of the Umayyads and justice and monotheism are the doctrines of the Alawis.

The earliest supporters and advocates of human liberty and free will during the Umayyad period were Ma'bad al-Juhani, an Iraqi and a Syrian known as Ghaylan of Damascus. These two persons were known for their honesty, integrity and faith. Ma'bad took part in the uprising of Ibn al-Ash'ath and was killed by Hajjaj. Ghaylan was hanged by order of Hisham ibn Abd al-Malik, who received a report about what he preached.

In his history of scholastic theology Shibli Nu'mani says:

"Though the stage was now fully set for the eruption of schisms in Islam, they started under political impetus. As during the Umayyad period injustice and tyranny were rampant, naturally the people were agitated and commotion existed everywhere. But whenever anybody made any complaint, the partisans of the government tried to silence him by saying that everything was ordained by Allah and none should utter a word against His will. We believe that good fortune and ill fortune both are from Allah".

Ma'bad Juhani was a very bold and frank man. One day he asked his teacher, Hasan Basri, if the question of fate and destiny as raised by the Umayyads was right. Hasan said: "They are the enemies of Allah. They are liars".

The Abbasids were the political enemies of the Umayyads. Their policy was different. Some of them, especially Mamun and Mu'tasim supported the Mu'tazilities who believed in human liberty. Still a new leaf was turned from the time of Mutawakkil, and official support was given to the doctrine of predestination. Since then the Ash'arite creed became popular in the Muslim world.

There is no doubt that the popularity and influence of the Ash'arties had a great impact on the Muslim world. Though the other sects, such as the Shi'ah did not officially follow them, yet even they could not escape from being influenced by them. The Shi'ah doctrine differs from that of the Ash'arites, though it is not in cent per cent agreement with that of the Mu'azilites also. Anyhow in the Shi'ah literature in Arabic and Persian there is not so much mention of human liberty as of man's being subject to his destiny, though the Imams of the Holy Family have expressly declared that the belief in fate is not on the whole inconsistent with the idea of human volition.

The words, fate and destiny have become awful and frightening because with the domination of the Ash'arite school in the Muslim world and it's influenced over Islamic literature, these words have become synonymous with compulsion, lack of liberty and illogical control of human actions and behavior by an invisible force.

CHAPTER 3

Onslaught of Christian Europe on Islam

This aspect of the question provided a pretext to the Christians of Europe to assert that the main cause of the decadence of the Muslims is their belief in fate and destiny and that Islam is a predestinarian system which totally deprives man of his liberty and volition. While in Europe, Sayyid Jamal al-Din al-Afghani (1839-1897), took notice of this criticism and replied to it in his articles. In the introduction of an article he said that if the spirit of a people was not pure and congenial, even the pure tenet of its faith were bound to be perverted. In their new form they only would add to its misery and error. They would be converted into a force which would lead it to further wicked deeds.

He further said:

"The true doctrine of fate and destiny has been greatly misunderstood by the uninformed. The Europeans are mistaken when they say that a nation believing in this doctrine losses its boldness, courage and other good qualities, and that all the undesirable qualities of the present day Muslims are the outcome of this very belief. Today the

Muslims are poor. They are politically and militarily weaker than the European nations. Corruption, malice, dissension, disunity, ignorance, lack of insight and satisfaction with a subsistence level of living are rampant among them. They are not concerned with their progress and are not keen to pushing back their enemy. The ruthless armies of the enemy are attacking them from all sides, but they are not perturbed. They submit to every humiliation. They have fallen into slumber and left the treasures of wealth and independence to their enemies and the aliens."

He continued to say:

"The Europeans ascribe to the Muslims all the evils we have enumerated. According to them all these are the products of a belief in fate and destiny. They say if the Muslims will continue to stick to this belief for some time more, they will be doomed."

He added:

"The Europeans do not differentiate between a belief in fate and destiny and a belief in predestination according to which man has no liberty of action."

Mental Complex

From the foregoing it should not be concluded that the question of fate and destiny and that of predestination and free will have arisen among the Muslims for any social or political reasons. As we will explain later these questions are primarily a scientific problem, a philosophical unknown, and a mental complex. They arise for every individual and every nation which is capable of thinking over general questions. Probably there is no nation in the world which has not thought over them in one way or other.

Material Philosophy and Destiny

Some people are under the impression that this dilemma presents itself only to those who believe in religion, and the materialists are not faced with any such problem.

This is a false impression. The people having the material way of thinking are also faced with this problem, though with a little difference.

According to the law of causation every event and every phenomenon is the product of one or more causes, and that cause (or causes) in turn is the product of some other cause or causes. It is an indisputable corollary of this law that in the presence of the relevant cause the effect must appear and in the absence of it, the appearance of the effect is impossible. The materialists accept this relationship between a cause and its effect and consider it to be the basis of their material philosophy. Now obviously the human acts like all other phenomena must be governed by this law. They cannot be an exception to it. If that is so where can theory of free will and human liberty stand?

This is why we see that in all old and new philosophical systems the problem of compulsion and free will exists quite well. As we will explain later, some variation in the nature of the problem makes no substantial difference. In fact the belief in fate and destiny has certain advantages that are missing in the belief in physical compulsion.

Oneness of Allah and His Purity

The dilemma faced by the theologians and the religious philosophers was that they on the one hand believed that nothing could happen without the Will of Allah and on the other knew that nothing dirty or wicked could be ascribed to Him. Consequently they wavered. Some of them held that human acts and deeds, which could often be dirty or wicked, were not subject to the Will of Allah. Others maintained that everything was subject to His Will because He alone is the Primary Cause of the existence of everything.

It is reported that Ghaylan of Damascus who was a supporter of Free Will once said to the well-known scholar, Rabi'ah al-Ray: "Do you think that Allah likes to be disobeyed?" What he meant was the Rabi'ah believed that even the sins occurred by the Will of Allah. Rabi'ah at once resorted: "It is you who believe that Allah is disobeyed against His will". He meant that according to the belief of Ghaylan it was possible that something might happen which Allah did not will.

Once while Abu Ishaq Isfarayini was sitting with Sahib Ibn Ubbad, Qazi Abd al-Jabbar, a Mu'tazilite arrived. As soon as Qazi Abd al-Jabbar who denied the generality of fate and destiny, saw Abu Ishaq, he remarked: "Glorified be He who is free from every indecent thing". He meant that Allah was above—that indecent things be ascribed to Him. He alluded to the belief of Abu Ishaq that everything was from Allah which necessarily meant that indecent things were also from Him. Abu Ishaq retorted without hesitation and said: "Glorified be He in Whose domain nothing happens except that which He Wills". He meant that according to the belief of the Qazi, the things which Allah did not will could happen. Such a belief went against the cardinal tenet of monotheism.

As we have pointed out earlier, so long as this question was not affected by political and social motives, it was purely a philosophical problem. A certain section of the people could not acquiesce in the belief that evils and vices were imputable to Allah. They considered Him to be far above such things. Another section which was more familiar with the idea of monotheism, believed that in the universe everything was sustained by Allah and hence the existence of anything capable of taking an independent action against His Will was untenable. This difference of view gave rise to divergent creeds.

Each section tried to prove the correctness of its idea by leveling criticism against that of the other but without being able to answer the objections raised against its own point of view. A reference to the books of scholastic theology will make what we mean clear. The fact is that neither of the doctrines of fate defensible in the form in which they are enunciated by their respective exponents. If both sections could understand that what they say is only partially true, the dispute would have been settled. In fact the belief in fate, destiny and monotheism does not necessarily mean predestinarianism, nor does the doctrine of free will imply the negation of fate.

CHAPTER 4

Literal Meanings of '*Qadha*' and '*Qadar*'

In Arabic the words '*qadha*' and '*qadar*' are used for fate and destiny. The word, '*qadha*' means to decide; to settle; to judge. A '*qadhi*' (judge) is called so because he decides judicially between the litigants. In the Qur'an this word has been used frequently with reference to both man and Allah. It has been used in the sense of giving a final verdict and taking a decisive action.

The word, '*qadr*' means to measure; to assess; and to determine. It also has been used in the Qur'an frequently.

The events of the world are said to be dividedly decided because they take place within the Knowledge of Allah and are subject to His Will. They are said to the divinely determined because their time, place and nature are determined in accordance with a system fixed by Allah.

We skip over the questions raised and the terminology used in this connection by the scholastic theologians for what they have dwelt on mostly relates to such questions as Allah's Knowledge and its degrees.

The only question which we may take up in the course of our

present study is that the events taking place in the world may be looked at from three angles. Either we may say that they have no past. In other words, an event which takes place at any time is not related to anything preceding it, nor does its existence depend on anything prior to it. Its temporal and spatial characteristics and its scope and extent were not determined in the past.

If this hypothesis is accepted, there is no meaning of destiny. According to this theory the destiny of a thing is not predetermined at the stage of the existence of another thing preceding it, for there is no existential link between the two. If we accept this view, we will have to deny the principle of causation totally and will have to explain unscientifically all events as mere accidents.

However the principle of causation and the existence of an essential link between various events are fact, which are undeniable. Everything acquires its inevitability and its existential characteristics from some other thing or things preceding it. The principle of causation is in a way the basis of all human knowledge.

Another possibility is that we should maintain that every event has a cause, but deny that every cause necessitates a particular effect and that every effect can emanate only from a particular cause. In this case we can believe that the whole universe has not more than one cause and agent and that is Allah. All existing things and all events emanate from Him directly. His Will attaches to every event separately. His Will and Knowledge of everything is independent of His Will and Knowledge of any other thing.

In this case we can say that there is no agent except Allah. He knows from eternity that such and such event will take place at such and such time, and that event must perforce come into existence at that particular moment. No other factor affects the existence of that event. Human deeds and acts also being a kind of event, emanate direct from the Will and Knowledge of Allah. The human will and power are only a facade or a mere illusion, and not actually effective in bringing about any event.

This is true predestinarianism, that is the view which if held by a person or a nation, will certainly lead them to ruination.

This view, besides the practical and social evils which it entails is logically absurd. There is no doubt that it does not stand to reason. The system of causation or the connection of causes and effects is undeniable. Not only physical sciences and perceptual and experimental observations prove the existence of a system of causes and effects, but also there are very strong philosophical arguments in support of it. The Holy Qur'an also endorses the doctrine of causation.

According to the third view, all the events in the world are governed by a system of causation. Every event acquires its inevitability and its existential characteristics from the causes proceeding to it. There exists an unbreakable link between the past, the present and the future, that is between every phenomenon and its preceding causes.

According to this view the destiny of everything in existence is in the hands of some other thing which is its cause, which has necessitated it and has made it inevitable. It is the case which determines the existential characteristics of its effect. Every cause in its turn is the effect of another cause. And so on.

The acceptance of the general principle of causation means the acceptance of the view that every event acquires its inevitability and its characteristics of shape, size and quality from

its cause or causes. It makes no difference whether we believe or
not in a religion and the First Cause, that is the source of every
determination.

If this view is upheld then as far as the question of destiny is
concerned, there will be no difference between a theist and an
atheist. The belief in destiny is corollary of the belief in the
principle of causation. The only difference is that an atheist looks
at the question from material angle only. He believes that the
destiny of everything in existence is determined by the causes are
not conscious of the work they do. On the other hand, a theist
maintains that at the long end of the chain there are certain causes
which are conscious of their work and their own characteristics.
The theists call such causes the 'Book', the 'Tablet' and the 'Pen',
whereas the materialistic school has nothing worthy of these
names.

Predestination

From the foregoing discussion it is clear that a belief in fate and
destiny and that every event, including human deeds and acts, is
determined by Divine decrees, does not necessarily mean
predestination. It would have certainly meant so, had we believed
that man and his will have no role in this respect. As hinted
earlier, the Divine Being does not influence the events of the
world direct. That is absolutely impossible. He necessitates the
existence of a thing through its particular causes only. That
everything is decreed by Allah simply means that the system of
causation is subject to His Will and Knowledge. As already
pointed out, the acceptance of the principle of causation implies
that the destiny of everything in existence depended on the causes
preceding it. It does not matter whether we believe that the system

of causation emanates from the Divine Will or presume that it exists independently, for its independence or dependence does not in any way affect human destiny.

It is foolish to hold that the doctrine of predestination has any relation to the belief in fate and destiny, or to criticize this belief on that account.

There is absolutely no such thing as destiny if it means the denial of an inevitable connection between the causes and their effects. It will amount to the denial of human liberty and volition. In theology very strong and convincing arguments have been advanced to prove the baselessness of such an idea.

But if destiny means a link of inevitability between an event and its causes, then its existence is an undeniable fact. Anyhow, it should be remembered that the belief in destiny is not peculiar to the theists. Every school of thought which believes in the general system of causation has to accept the existence of this link of inevitability. The only difference is that the theists hold that the chain of causes at a dimension other than that of time or place ends at the Essential Being, Who is self-existent. Thus all inevitabilities and determinations stop at a particular point.

Anyhow, this difference neither proves nor disproves the doctrine of predestination.

CHAPTER 5

Freedom and Liberty

There is no doubt that if the divinely appointed fate is supposed to be related to the events direct without the intervention of the causes, human freedom and liberty will have no meaning. Now the next question is whether it is possible to accept the general principle of causation and the principle of human liberty simultaneously. Are they not inconsistent? It appears that the only way to believe in human freedom and liberty is to consider human will and acts not to be related to any external causes and to accept the first theory out of the three theories mentioned above.

Many ancient and modern thinkers are of the view that the principle of causation is inconsistent with human liberty, and hence they believe in free will not related to any cause. In other words they are the proponents of mere chance and accident.

We have established in the foot-notes of our book, *Principles of Philosophy*, vol. III that the general principle of causation is undeniable and it admits of no exception. The denial of relation between human will and external causes would amount to saying that the acts of man are totally beyond his control. Thus instead of adding to human liberty, we will be diminishing it further, by accepting the view.

Man has been created free. That means that he has been endowed with intellect, will and thinking power. As far as his intentional acts are concerned, he is not like a stone which if dropped from above will automatically fall on the ground under the pressure of the gravity of the earth. Nor is he like a plant which has only a very limited course open to it and is only subject to the laws of growth and decay. Similarly he is not like a mere animal which works only instinctively. Man always finds himself at cross roads, but is not in any way compelled to choose anyone of them. Other roads are not closed to him. The choice depends upon his will and personal thinking. It is entirely up to him to choose a particular way.

His choice will be the outcome of his personality, his moral and spiritual qualities, his previous raining, his hereditary traits and his intellectual capacity. His happy or unhappy future depends on these qualities and the choice he makes consequently.

Fire burns; water submerges; a plant grows and an animal walks. They all work. The difference is that they do not choose, whereas man chooses. He decides what he wants to do and which way he wants to go. His work is subject to his own personal desire.

Inevitable and Non-Inevitable

In the reports and traditions, fate and destiny have been described as revocable and irrevocable. There are hints in the Qur'an also to that effect. It appears that there are two kinds of fate and destiny, one inevitable and unalterable and the other non-inevitable and alterable.

Now the question is: what is the meaning of non-inevitable fate and destiny? Let us take any particular event in view. Have the Eternal Knowledge and Will of Allah attached to it? If they have not, there is no question of destiny. If they have, the event must take place, otherwise that would mean the nonconformity of the Divine Knowledge to the reality and the non-fruition of Allah's Will.

To be more precise we may say that destiny means the emanation of all the required causes from the Knowledge and Will of Allah, who is the First Cause. As we know, the general law of causation necessitates inevitability. This law requires that the occurrence of an event should be sure under its own special temporal and spatial conditions and its nonoccurrence also should be certain in other circumstances. The finality of the scientific rules is due to this very law.

Man can make scientific predictions to the extent of his limited knowledge of the causes. Therefore the decision of fate and destiny which determines the occurrence of the events through the system of causation, must be regarded as conclusive. As such to divide destiny into inevitable and non-inevitable appears to be meaningless.

At this stage a dilemma arises. Either we should, like the Ash'arites, believe in destiny in its limited sense only or say that it is absolutely unalterable and that man has no power to change it; or like the Mu'tazilites deny its role at least as far as human acts and deeds are concerned. Let us see how we can resolve this dilemma.

It may incidentally be said that just as the Ash'arite view implies the denial of man's liberty and his control of his destiny, the Mu'tazilite view also besides being contrary to the monotheistic principles and the concept of divine knowledge, does not serve any useful purpose from the angle of human freedom. Even if we do not accept the fate and destiny in their divine sense, what shall we do of their material concept, according to which every event in the world is controlled by the system of causation? That also amounts to compulsion.

Can we deny the working of the law of causation, at least in the case of free agent, that is man. Some modern European philosophers also have expressed the same view as was held by the Mu'tazilites. They have talked of free will not subject to the law that it is applicable only to the material world composed of atoms, and is not applicable to the spiritual world or even to the internal world of the atoms. We cannot here dwell on the law of causation. Anybody interested in its detailed discussion may refer to our book, *The Principles of Philosophy and the Method of Realism*, vol. III, footnotes.

Here it is enough to say that the modern philosophers have denied the generality of the law of causation, because they think that it is an experimental law and as such have considered those cases to be out of its scope in which human experiments have not been able to discover a definite relationship of cause and effect.

In fact it is a big mistake to presume that all scientific laws, rules, all mental conceptions are based on human perception and experiment. This is a mistake which has been committed by many Western systems of philosophy and from them it has passed to their Eastern followers.

In short, there is no way of denying the law of general causation, and with its acceptance the problem of the non-inevitability of destiny remains as it is, whether we believe or not in its divine aspect. Briefly speaking the problem is that all events including human acts and deeds are bound to acquire inevitability through their causes which determine their specifications and characteristics. The system of causation itself means inevitability and certainty. Hence the question of a change in destiny does not arise.

All the believers in "the general principle of causation" and they include the materialists, who believe in determinism and at the same time hold that the destiny is changeable and that man controls his destiny, are faced with this dilemma. Therefore the Mu'tazilite theory of the denial on the view that all the events of the world are not subject to Divine Will and that Divine Knowledge is not the source of the entire system of the universe, serves no purpose.

Impossible Fantasy

If the alterability of destiny and its non-inevitability are construed to mean that Divine Will and Knowledge necessitate one thing and then an independent factor arises and necessitates something contrary to it, or that an independent factor can change Divine Will and Knowledge, then obviously such an idea is absurd.

Similarly it is also not possible that the law of causation should necessitate one thing and a factor independent to it may nullify its effect.

The fact is that all factors in the world flow from the Knowledge and Will of Allah. Every factor is a manifestation of His Will and Knowledge and an instrument of the implementation of what He has decreed. At the same time every factor which we can think of is subject to the law of causation. It cannot be imagined that a factor which is in itself a manifestation of the Will of Allah and is subject to the law of causation can ever go against what He has obtained.

Hence, a change of destiny in the sense that any factor can go against what has been divinely ordained or what the law of causation necessitates, is impossible.

What Is Possible

But a change in destiny in the sense that the factor bringing about the change should itself be a manifestation of what Allah has decreed, is possible. Though it may look rather queer, it is a fact that the destiny can be changed by another destiny.

It may look more surprising if we think of the divine aspect of fate and destiny, for a change in this aspect implies a change in the celestial world, in the angelic tablets and books and in the Divine Knowledge. So can Allah's Knowledge still undergo a change? The surprise reaches its height when we admit that certain terrestrial affairs, especially human will and actions cause changes in the celestial world and the angelic record.

Is it not a fact that the terrestrial and material system emanates from the celestial system? Is it not a fact that the terrestrial world is inferior and the celestial world is superior? Is it not a fact that the human world is dominated by the angelic world? Is it still possible that a lower system, or at least a part of it, *viz.* the human world should influence a higher system and bring about changes in it, even if these changes also should take place in accordance with an appointed destiny? Here several remarkable questions crop up consecutively. Is the Knowledge of Allah changeable? Is a divine decree revocable? Can an inferior influence a superior?

The answer to these questions is in the affirmative. Yes, the Knowledge of Allah is changeable. In other words Allah has such knowledge also which is changeable. A divine decree is revocable. In other words Allah has decrees which are revocable. An inferior can influence a superior. A lower system, especially the will, desire and human acts can shake the higher world and cause changes in it. This is the highest form of man's control of his destiny.

We admit that this statement is surprising, but it is factual. This is that lofty question of *Bada'* which for the first time in human history was mentioned by the Qur'an:

> "*Allah creates whatever He wants (out of what was recorded previously) and records whatever He wants (that was not recorded previously) and with Him alone is the Mother Book*".

Sūrah Al-Ra'd, 13:39

The doctrine has no precedent in the field of human knowledge. Among the Muslim sects it is only the Twelver Shi'ahs who have been able to derive this truth from the sayings of the Imams of the Ahlul-Bayt and they are proud of this distinction.

We are unable to give a full explanation of this highly philosophical question in this brief book. It is enough to say that the question of *Bada'* has a Qur'anic basis. It is one of the most subtle philosophical subjects and only very few Shi'ah philosophers well-versed in the Qur'an have been able to reach its depth. They were able to do so in the light of the sayings of the Imams, especially those of Imam Ali, the Commander of the Faithful. Anyhow, it is obvious that in respect of such a subtle question reliance cannot be placed on the lay man's conception of it, which is nothing but absurd.

For the present we are mainly concerned with the question of the changeability of destiny. We have to see whether it is true that from material angle destinies are revocable and some others irrevocable. If so, how can this phenomenon be explained?

The things existing are of two kinds. Some of them do not have the possibility of having more than one kind of special existence, like the heavenly abstracts. Some others have such a possibility, like all visible and perceptible things. They are composed of some kind of matter and prepare the ground for coming into being of some other things. Natural matter can receive various forms and shapes. It can evolve. It grows, decays and decomposes. It is affected by various factors and under the impact of each one of them its state and quality changes. A seed sown in the soil grows and matures if it meets favorable climatic conditions, receives an appropriate amount of light and heat and its not affected by the pests. But its growth will naturally be hampered, if any of the necessary factors are lacking or the seed itself is damaged in any way. There are thousand and one if's in the case of any way. There are thousand and one if's in the case of any kind of natural matter. If this happens, the result will be that, and if that happens, the result will be something different. In other words, the effect varies as the causes vary.

As the heavenly abstracts do not have more than one kind of existence and are not influenced by divergent causes, their destiny is irrevocable and cannot undergo a change. Destiny is always determined by its causes. As in the case of the abstracts their causes are not changeable, their destiny also does not change. But the case of the non-abstracts is different. They are subject to the law of motion, and have countless forms and colours. They are always at cross-roads and have several possibilities. Hence their destiny is revocable.

In other words, one single destiny does not determine them. As we have said, the destiny of every effect is determined by its cause. As the non-abstracts can have many causes, they can have many destinies also. As each series of their causes is liable to be replaced by another series, their destiny cannot be firm. There will always be a possibility of the change in destiny with the change in the circumstances. If someone falls sick, there is no doubt that his disease is the result of some particular cause, which has brought about this particular destiny. Now suppose he takes some effective medicine. This medicine is another cause. It will produce a different destiny. If with the taking of medicine the disease disappears, that means that the destiny of the patient has changed. Suppose this particular patient is treated by two physicians and their diagnosis and prescription are different. While the treatment diagnosis and prescription are different, the treatment prescribed by one of them has a curative and healing effect, that of the other is lethal. In this case it may be said that two different destines are in store for this patient, and as he has an option to choose either of the treatments, it may be said that neither of his destines is irrevocable. Naturally his eventual choice will depend upon so many open and hidden factors. But the fact that he chooses one particular treatment, does not preclude the latent possibility of the choice of the other.

Hence it is clear that in many cases a number of destinies are operative and they can replace one another it a man suffering from a disease takes a medicine and recovers, he does so in accordance with his fate and destiny. Again if he does not take any medicine and continues to suffer, or takes a harmful medicine and dies, that is also perfectly in accordance with his fate and destiny.

Similarly if a man moves out of an infected area and saves himself from being affected by a disease, that is also owing to his fate and destiny. In short everything is within the purview of destiny and one can never escape it.

The point is that destiny is the source of all factors in the world, but in itself it is not a factor which may bring other factors into play. Every factor which comes into play is a manifestation of destiny and at the same time is subject to the general law of causation. As such, destiny cannot be a factor independent of other factors nor can it force any other factor to act in a particular way.

That is why the theory of predestination, which means compulsion by destiny, is not tenable. As we have said, destiny is the source of all factors, but in itself it is not a factor to bring into play any other factors. Hence, destiny cannot force man to do a thing. There is no doubt that certain manifestation of destiny can be compelling, but that compulsion is totally different from predestination which is supposed to influence human will direct as a negative factor to deter man from doing a thing or as a positive factor to force him to do it. In other words destiny is changeable because it necessitates the existence of a thing through its natural causes, which are manifold. The matter in this world is liable to be influenced by a number of causes simultaneously.

Naturally the position becomes different if like the Ash'arites we hold that causation is a mere illusion, or like the semi-Ash'arities believe that in exceptional circumstances the course of events is directly affected by fate and destiny. But such a fate and such a destiny do not exist, nor can they exist.

CHAPTER 6

Human Distinction

Human acts are among the events which have no definite and irrevocable destiny. They depend on thousand and one causes, including man's own will and choice. All the possibilities which exist in the case of inorganic material, plants and the instinctive acts of the animals, are valid in the case of man also. In addition he has intellect, will and choosing power.

Man for his own reasons and of his own will can abstain from doing a thing which is fully in keeping with his natural and animal instinct. Similarly without being compelled by any external forces he can do a thing which is totally against his nature, if he thinks that it is advisable to do that. Man like animals is influenced by his instinctive motives and emotional desires, but he is not tied to them. Even in the presence of all the factors which compel an animal to act instinctively, man is free to use his will power and to decide whether he should or should not take a particular action. His performance of an act depends on like an executive authority. That is why man influences his destiny as a free agent. He is always at liberty to do or not to do a thing.

Anyhow, his liberty does not mean that he is not subject to the law of causation, or he can evade it. In fact human liberty does not mean man's freedom from the law of causation. In contrast such a freedom will actually amount to compulsion, for practically there is no difference between man's being forced by a particular factor to act against his will, and the act itself not being dependent on has liberty and freedom, we mean that his acts emanate from his will with the approval of his power of discrimination and no-external factor, whether it is destiny or anything else, forces him to do a thing against his desire.

In short all causes are manifestations of the divinely ordained fate and destiny. The number of imaginable destines in respect of an event will be corresponding with the number of the causes and the alternatives which can be imagined. The particular course which an event takes will be in accordance with a divinely ordained destiny, and the course which it does not take will also be in accordance with a divinely ordained destiny.

CHAPTER 7

A Glance at the Early Period of Islam

The Holy Prophet was asked about the amulets used for seeking a cure, (Ghazzali reports that the question was about both the spell and the medicine) whether they could forestall a divinely ordained destiny. In reply the Prophet said that they themselves were a part of destiny (*Bihar al-Anwar*). He meant to say that their healing effect was also divinely ordained.

Imam Ali was sitting under the shade of a bent wall. He moved from that place and went to another wall. Someone said to him: "O Commander of the Faithful! Do you flee from a divinely ordained destiny?" He said: "Yes, I feel from one destiny to another".[3] In other words, he said that if he sat under a dilapidated wall and it fell on him, that would be in accordance with a divinely ordained destiny, for it is within the normal course of a sequence of causes and effects that a man sitting under a tottering wall should suffer. Similarly it was also in accordance with a divinely ordained destiny that he should be safe, if he moved away.

---

[3] Shaykh Sadduq, *Tawhid*.

It is possible that in the course of another sequence of cause and effect, the same person may be confronted with some other danger. If that happens, that also will be in accordance with a divinely ordained fate and destiny.

Anyway, to keep oneself away from a danger amounts to fleeing from one divinely ordained destiny to another.

History of Islam on the whole indicates that the Muslims of early era had a firm belief in fate and destiny. They did not see any inconsistency between their being masters of their own destiny and their belief in this doctrine. They considered it to be an indisputable fact that not only destiny was changeable but also that all changes were a part of an overall destiny. They had a firm belief in destiny, but never believed in compulsion or predestination. Therefore they did not become lethargic and insensitive nor did they leave anything to their fate. They always asked Allah for the best destiny, because they knew that various destinies existed in every case.

It may look surprising that they asked for the best destiny but not the best of what had been destined, as is borne out by the wordings of their prayer. It is all the more surprising that even the simple-minded Muslims were conscious of this subtle difference.

Ibn Abi al-Hadid in his commentary on the *Nahjal-Balaghah* says: 'While on his way to Syria Umar ibn al-Khattab received a report that plague had broken out there. He consulted his companions whether he should visit the affected town. Most of them advised him not to take this risk. But Abu Ubaydah ibn al-Jarrah said: "O Commander of the Faithful! Do you flee from a divinely ordained destiny?" "Yes, I flee from one divinely ordained destiny to another", said Umar. At this stage a man claimed that he had heard the Prophet saying: "Do not enter a town where plague is raging. But if you are already in it, do not leave it". Umar, who was somewhat hesitant before hearing this *ḥadīth*, decided not to visit the place.'

The Shi'ah and the Sunni reports on the whole indicate that the Holy Prophet (ṣ) raised the question of fate and destiny before his companions. Similarly Imam Ali on several occasions talked about it. It is remarkable that they dealt with this question with such a skill that it did not lead the early Muslims to predestinarianism, nor did it shake their self-confidence.

The reports of their sayings and doings which have reached us, clearly bear out this fact. Later when the Muslim scholastic theologians started discussing and analyzing this question, they could not distinguish between a belief in destiny and in predestinarianism. Since then the confusion is continuing with a result that a belief during the past fourteen centuries, very few scholars have been able to make a clear distinction between the two doctrines.

CHAPTER 8

Qur'an is the Source of Teachings

The Holy Qur'an is the original source of the doctrine which requires man to believe in fate. At the same time it tells him that they are the masters of their destiny. The Qur'an alludes to people the plurality of destiny also.

> *"It is He who has created you from clay, and then has decreed a term for you to live. There is another fixed term with Him".*
>
> Sūrah Al-An'ām, 6:2

The Qur'an does mention the Protected Tablet, the Eternal Book and the ordained destiny. It says:

> *"There is nothing green or withered, but is recorded in a clear Book".*
>
> Sūrah Al-Ḥadīd, 57:22

But it also says:

"Every moment He brings about a new manifestation of His Power".

Sūrah al-Raḥmān, 55:29

Someone asked the Holy Prophet (ṣ):

"Has Allah finished what we are busy with, or are we doing something new". The Prophet (ṣ) said: "He has finished and He has not".[4]

Invariability in Nature

We have said that the religious leaders have mentioned two kinds of destiny. We have also said that the destiny of the heavenly abstracts, unlike that of the things existing in nature, is always irrevocable. Let us now add that in nature also irrevocable destiny exists. In other words there are events which must take place in a fixed manner. For example in nature everything in existence is preceded by its non-existence. Everything must emanate from some other existing thing. These are examples of an irrevocable destiny. Every natural thing must perish, unless it is converted into an immaterial being. This is another example of an irrevocable destiny. All the things that exist in this world reach a stage at which they cannot change their course. Either they should follow the prescribed course or must vanish.

For example, through the union of a male-sperm with a female ovum one single cell is formed. It lays down the foundation of the hereditary characteristics and temperament of the coming child. These hereditary traits are bound to affect his future destiny. Had the union of this particular sperm taken place

---

[4] Commentary on *Usul al-Kafi* by Mulla Sadra.

with the ovum of some other female, a different child with a different temperament and some different characteristics would have been formed. But once an embryo has been formed, it is not possible to change its characteristics. At this stage the destiny has become definite and irrevocable at later stages. That is why, in the language of religion mother's womb has been called a "table of fate and destiny".

Unchangeable Systems

The laws and the systems governing the world are also unchangeable. The things existing in nature are constantly changing, but the natural systems governing them are firm. They do not undergo a change. The things develop and evolve. They take various courses. They sometimes attain almost perfection and sometimes remain stagnant. Sometimes they march speedily and sometimes slowly. But the natural systems neither change nor develop.

The Qur'an calls these unchangeable systems the divine practice.

> "The same was the way of Allah in respect of those who passed away earlier. And you will not find the way of Allah undergoing a change".

Sūrah Al-Aḥzāb, 33:63

It is an unchangeable divine practice that the final success pertains to the pious, and the earth belongs to the righteous.

Allah in the Holy Qur'an says:

> "Indeed We have written in the Psalms, after the Torah had

been given: The righteous among My slaves shall inherit the earth".

Sūrah Al-Anbiyā', 21:105

"The earth belongs to Allah. He gives it to whom He pleases. Happy shall be the end of the pious".

Sūrah Al-A'rāf, 7:128

It is an unchangeable divine practice that Allah does not change the general condition of a people unless and until they themselves make an effort to change it.

"Allah never changes the condition of a nation unless it (first) changes what is in its heart".

Sūrah Al-Ra'd, 13:11

It is an unchangeable divine practice that a people always gets that form of government which it deserves in accordance with its spiritual, moral and intellectual conditions.

"Thus we make the wrong-doers friends of each other because of their own doings".

Sūrah Al-An'ām, 6:129

It is an unchangeable divine practice that easy-going and luxuriously living licentious people are ruined.

"When We intend to destroy a township, We first warn those of its people who live an easy life. If they persist in their wickedness there, they become liable to punishment. Then We totally annihilate them".

Sūrah Al-Isrā', 17:16

It is an unchangeable divine practice that the people having faith and doing right deeds are always successful in the struggle for survival and they come to power in the world.

> *"Allah has promised those of you who believe and do good deeds that He will surely give them power on the earth as He gave to those who were before them to succeed, and that He will surely establish for them their religion which He has approved for them. He shall give them peace and security after a period of uneasiness".*

> Sūrah Al-Nūr, 24:55

It is an unchangeable divine practice that injustice and tyranny lead to ruin and devastation.

> *"We destroyed the people of all those towns because they were unjust, and we appointed a fixed time for their destruction".*

> Sūrah Al-Kahf, 18:59

The Holy Prophet (ṣ) has said:

"A regime can continue with unbelief, but not with tyranny".

Other Theories

According to the explanation given by us, the fate and destiny are divided into revocable and irrevocable in accordance with the special circumstances of the things concerned. A thing which has more than one possibility and is affected by various causes in various ways, will have several possible destinies. Their number will depend upon the number of the relevant causes. The destiny of a thing which is affected by more than one course is regarded as revocable. In contrast the destiny of a thing having not more than one possibility and having only one possible course will be irrevocable. In other words, the question of revocability and irrevocability is considered from the angle of capability, that is whether a thing is capable of having only one destiny or more than one. That is why the destiny of the heavenly abstracts which lack the potentiality of more than one future and similarly that of certain things existing in nature which do not have more than one phenomena capable of having more than one future is revocable. That sums up the position which regard to revocable and irrevocable destiny.

This question has been interpreted differently also. Some scholars hold that the destiny of the realities which cannot be changed by man is irrevocable, and the destiny of the realities which can be changed by him is revocable. For example, it is not possible for man, at least at present, to bring about any change in the atmospheric conditions with regard to summer, winter, rain, snow, wind *etc.* or to change the general conditions of the earth with regard to earthquakes, storms, floods *etc.* These are the happenings which take place whether man wants them or not. Hence the destiny in respect of such things is irrevocable. As for the social conditions, they can be changed and reformed. The divinely ordained destiny in their case is revocable.

This interpretation is incorrect, for there is no reason why we should presume that human power and potentialities are the basis of the revocability or irrevocability of destiny. Moreover, the language of the religious reports and *hadīths* also does not support this interpretation.

Some other scholars judge the revocability and irrevocability of a destiny by the realization and the non-realization of its prerequisite conditions. We have already said that certain things have several possibilities and are associated with a number of causes. It depends on the working of these causes, what future shape they take. Every cause has a potential capacity of providing a particular destiny and every destiny depends on the realization of a particular cause. It is obvious that certain causes along with their prerequisite conditions are realized, while others are not. It is also obvious that the reason why certain causes are realized is that some other causes which give effect to them exist. Other causes are not realized because the causes which could give affect to them did not exist. The same applies to the third and the fourth degree of the causes and so on.

In short, the things, the causes of which come into existence, are irrevocably destined whereas the things the causes of which do not come into existence are revocably destined. Suppose a man according to his physical health expects to live for 150 years provided he looks after his health. If he does not, his expectation of the life will be reduced to one half of that period. Now suppose that man does not look after his health and dies at the age of 75. It will be right to say that this man was destined to have two ages, and both of them were conditional. The condition of only one of them was fulfilled.

The destiny, the condition of which has been fulfilled is irrevocable and that the condition of which has not been fulfilled is revocable.

The two destinies in this case may be compared to two rules of law applicable to a person under different circumstances. For example, the law says if an accused makes a confession of his crime, he will be sentenced to a certain term of imprisonment. But if he does not make a confession and there is no other evidence against him, he will be acquitted. Now if the accused makes a confession, he will definitely receive the punishment. That rule of law which says that the accused will be punished if he makes a confession has become irrevocable in respect of this particular man, and the other rule which says that the accused will be acquitted if he does not make a confession provided there is no other evidence against him, could not become so.

According to this explanation irrevocability in this case means the practical application of a provision of law. Otherwise the law itself as a general rule is firm and fixed in all cases. This world is governed by a series of laws which are fixed and unfailing. As a general rule, they are irrevocable and unexceptionable. For example, there is a definite law that the persons having a certain physical standard should live upto 150 years of age provided they take care of their health. It is also a definite law that if such persons do not take care of their life will be reduced to one half. These laws are the manifestations of divine practice. They form the lines according to which a destiny is appointed. Therefore it may be said that an irrevocable destiny is that law or universal practice the conditions of the applicability of which are not fulfilled.

This interpretation appears to be plausible in itself, and some religious passages may also be found to be alluding to it. But the terms of a revocable destiny and an irrevocable destiny as used in *ḥadīths* cannot be taken to have this sense. There can be no doubt that a revocable destiny means a changeable destiny. But, in the cases where the conditions of the applicability of a general law materialize, the possibility of a change does not still totally disappear. These cases could certainly take a different turn, and hence they do not lose their aspect of revocability.

According to another interpretation an irrevocable destiny is that which has been made binding by Allah, and which is indispensable. A revocable destiny is that in relation to which the Will of Allah is neutral or indifferent, or at least a question of inevitability is not involved in it. According to this view the case of destiny is similar to that of legal matters. A law giver does not declare every action to be imperative. Some actions are made obligatory. Some other remain permissible. Still some others may be declared desirable or a abominable. The same applies to factual matters also. An irrevocable destiny involves obligation, whereas a revocable one does not.

This interpretation is most unscientific. It actually amounts to the negation of fate and destiny, for it is impossible that the Will of Allah be neutral or indifferent to any event, or at least may not make it inevitable.

Similarly, it is also impossible that an event may not be subject to the law of causation or in the case of being subject to it there may be no question of compulsion and obligation in respect of it.

It is not a sound analogy to compare factual realities to conventional matters.

CHAPTER 9

Effect of Spiritual Factors

The forgoing examples of the causes and the factors affecting destiny were concerned only with the material factors and their effects. We took into consideration only the material and perceptible aspects of the events, for from material angle only these factors and their causative relations are worth consideration. But from spiritual angle and reality is not confined to matter and body and their physical reactions and susceptibilities. The world of events has a more complicated structure and there are many more factors which contribute to an occurrence.

From material angle it is material factors only which cause death, provide means of living and bring about health, happiness and success. It is material factors alone which prolong or damage health and ensure or destroy happiness. But from religious point of view there are other factors also, known as spiritual factors, which are working side by side with the material factors and which affect every aspect of life.

From spiritual point of view the world is a living and conscious unit. All human deeds produce reactions. It is not immaterial to be good or to be bad. Human deeds, whether good or bad produce certain reactions in the world and the individual concerned himself is sometimes affected by them during his lifetime.

To cause hurt to a living being, whether a man or an animal, especially to the persons of such privileged position as that of father, mother, teacher etc. brings about evil consequences in this very world. Requital is a natural system. The consequences and effects of the human deeds are a part of the manifestations of fate and destiny. The cases of the interrelation between the events and this phenomenon can be explained only by the doctrine that this world is a living and conscious unit. They cannot be explained by materialistic way of thinking.

In accordance with the spiritual thinking the world sees and hears. It listens to the cry of the living beings and responds to them. That is why prayer is an effective cause. It produces certain occurrences and prevents certain others. In other words, it is such a manifestation of fate and destiny which may determine the ultimate lot of an event.

The Holy Qur'an says:

When My bondmen question you concerning Me, then surely I am nigh. I answer the prayer of the supplicant when he cries unto Me".

Sūrah Al-Baqarah, 2:186

The Holy Prophet (ṣ) has said:

"Prayer changes even confirmed destiny".

Similarly charity is another factor which is a manifestation of fate and destiny and which is effective in changing the fortune.

On the whole, vice and virtue, repentance and impenitence, justice and injustice, prayer and curse and the like are things which affect human beings in regard to their life, health, means of living etc.

Imam Sadiq has said:

"The number of those who die because of committing sins is larger than the number of those who die their natural death, and the number of those who live because of doing good deeds is larger than the number of those who live because of their real age".

The idea is that the sins shorten life and the good deeds prolong is. They change the appointed time and death. They change the destiny though, as we have pointed out earlier, this change is also a part of the divinely ordained destiny.

Here we cannot enter into the discussion as to how the spiritual matters affect the material things and how the system of causation works in this respect. That will require deep philosophical discussion. Anyhow, the philosophical view expressed in this connection agrees with what is indicated by the religious texts. In the present context we do not propose to dwell on the conditions under which the spiritual causes, such as prayer and charity and similarly injustice, tyranny and infringement of the rights of others are effective and create reactions. Perhaps a voluminous book can be complied on the cases of human experience in this connection.

At present we only want to point out that the sequence of causes and effects in the world is not confined to material and perceptible phenomena.

CHAPTER 10

When a Divine Decree Comes,
Man Feels Helpless

Many reports from the Holy Prophet (ṣ) and the Imams say that when a divine decree comes, the whole system of caution, especially the faculties of thinking and reasoning cease to work. This point has been depicted in Persian and Arabic literature also.

In the book of ḥadīth, *Al-Jami'-as-Saghir* a number of Prophetic sayings to this effect have been quoted. One ḥadīth says:

> "When Allah wants to carry out his decree, he wrests the power of reasoning and understanding from the people. They repent when this power is restored to them afterwards".

In the *Tuhaf-ul-Uqul* Imam Reza is reported to have said:

> "When Allah wants his decree to be carried out, He wrests their thinking power from the people concerned. After the decree has been carried out this power is restored to each one of them. Then they wonder how it was that such a thing happened".

The famous mystic poet of Iran, Moulawi says:

> "When a divine decree comes,
> the power of understanding quits.
> Allah alone knows what He proposes".

> "When a divine decree comes,
> you cease to see deep.
> Then you cannot distinguish between a friend and a foe".

> "When a divine decree come,
> the physician loses his skill.
> His medicine does harm instead of being beneficial".

A difficulty about all such statements is that they describe fate and destiny as a force invalidating the general principal of causation and as a factor stronger than all other factors. This view is contradictory to what we have said that Allah does not decree anything to happen except through the normal course of causation. The wording of the *ḥadīths* also supports what we have said. A *ḥadīth* says:

> "Allah declines to carry out the affairs of the world except through their causes. He has appointed a cause for everything. Every cause has a reason behind it. Every reason is a piece of knowledge and every piece of knowledge has an eloquent door".

> Majma'ul-Bahrayn

Another difficulty is that these statements are contradictory to the general rule expressly mentioned in the Qur'an that everything is governed by fate and destiny and there is nothing which may be outside of their area of control. If everything and every event is governed by destiny, then divine destiny must every moment be operative. As such there is no meaning of saying "When a divine decree comes".

Hence the contents of the above-mentioned *ḥadīth* and the verses are not only inconsistent with the generality of the principal of causation, but are also repugnant to the comprehensiveness of fate and destiny. They indicate that a divine decree is operative only occasionally and when it is, everything else ceases to work. Men lose their power of understanding. Eyes stop to see. Medicines are no longer effective.

Now what should we conclude? Should we think that these *ḥadīths* and reports are spurious and have been fabricated by the predestinarians or is it possible that they have a sound interpretation?

In our opinion these *ḥadīths* and reports have a sense which is not inconsistent either with the principle of causation or with the comprehensiveness of fate and destiny.

They are actually applicable to those cases in which spiritual causes overshadow the material ones.

We have already said that the material causes are not the only effective causes. The overall system of causation consists of various kinds of causes, some of which are open and some hidden. Just as some of the material causes make some other material causes ineffective, similarly on some special occasions all material causes are put out of action under the impact of some spiritual ones.

Those who look at the material and perceptible causes only, do not know that there are thousands of other causes also and when they are in operation, they make the material causes ineffective.

The Qur'an itself refers to this point in a lucid and forceful manner. Describing the events of the Battle of Badr, it says:

"When you met the pagans' army, Allah made them appear fewer in your eyes and you appear fewer in their eyes so that His miracle of granting you (an incredible) victory could easily be fulfilled. To Allah do all things return".

Sūrah Al-Anfāl, 8:44

This incident was a case in which the spiritual causes got the better of the material causes. There exists a higher world order, that protects a community, which because of its excellent behaviour becomes entitled to divine support, against another community which deserve disgrace and ruin. The first community is helped though it may be lacking resources and the second community is condemned though it may be having everything at its disposal.

The Holy Qur'an says:

"If someone trusts Allah, He will suffice Him. He will surely bring about what He decrees. Allah has set a measure for everything".

Sūrah Al-Ṭalāq, 65:3

In this verse it has been expressly said that Allah has set a measure for everything. Nothing takes place haphazardly. In other words the system of causation has been recognized. At the same time it has been emphatically said that Allah brings. His Command to pass. In other words, where there is a question of spiritual relations or invisible Divine succour, the visible causes are made ineffective.

CHAPTER 11

Divine Destiny and Material Compulsion

Difference between the Two Doctrines

We have already said that the materialists and some Christians have used the question of fate and destiny as a weapon in their attack on Islam. They say that an essential result of the belief in destiny and fate is that man should consider himself to be powerless and unable to build a better society.

As we have said this misunderstanding is due to the fact that the difference between a belief in fate and destiny and predestinarianism has been ignored. According to the doctrine of predestination man has no liberty and no will of his own. He has no real control over what he says or does. His own moral and temperamental qualities have no bearing on his destiny. But according to the doctrine of fate and destiny, the Divine Will and Knowledge do not necessitate anything except through the system of cause and effect. It is unbecoming of the uniqueness and greatness of Allah that He should attach His Will and Knowledge to a thing direct without employing the medium of causes. Hence His Knowledge and Will attach to man's actions and deeds, his success and failure only through this medium. Allah has destined man to be free and to be a master of his destiny. As far as human liberty is concerned, there is no difference between the views of the religionists and the materialists. As a matter of fact, if the inevitability of the occurrence of an event through its cause automatically means compulsion and helplessness of man, then this is a view which is held by both. But if it does not mean that, and actually it does not, then again there is no difference between the two schools. Hence any criticism of the Islamic belief by the materialists and others who believe in the law of causation is simply based on misunderstanding and lack of knowledge.

But let us add that from another angle there is a very vital and remarkable difference between the two schools. The belief in fate and destiny as taught by religion leads to hope and extraordinary greater effort. But this is not true of the materialistic thinking. This is the real difference between the two schools.

As already stated, the effective factors which collectively constitute the world causes and are considered to be the manifestations of fate and destiny are not all material. They include spiritual causes also which are also a part of the effective factors and play a role in changing destiny.

According to this view a number of non-material forces are part of the world order. For example, the support of justice and equity is a spiritual force. This world is in existence because of justice and as a result of the efforts of those who defend its cause. Their efforts are not wasted.

The Holy Qur'an says:

"Believers, if you help Allah's cause, He will help you and will make you stand firmly".

Sūrah Muḥammad, 47:7

"Surely Allah defends those who are true. Allah does not like any treacherous ingrateful man".

Sūrah Al-Ḥajj, 22:38

"Surely whoever helps Allah's cause, shall he helped by Him. Surely Allah is Strong, Mighty".

Sūrah Al-Ḥajj, 22:40

Another force in the world is trust in Allah. Trust in Allah means that one should pursue the right path with determination and without faltering. Allah protects him who pursues the right goal without any regard to his own personal gain, who performs his duty selflessly and who has confidence in divine help.

These are the examples of some of the special forces at work in the world. Form religious point of view they are a part of the system of causation and manifestations of fate and destiny.

Therefore a sound belief in divinely ordained destiny leads the believer to correct action and makes him confident of the results. From materialistic point of view the rules of morality do not affect the universal systems. In this respect virtue and vice, right and wrong, justice and injustice are all alike. The universal systems are neutral to the virtuous and the wicked. But from religious point of view, that is not so. Those who believe in justice and uprightness, also believe in Divine Wisdom, Divine Mercy and Divine Justice. They believe that he who seeks Allah's pleasure and follows the injunctions prescribed by Him, will be safe. Such a belief in divine destiny and divine sagacity resulting in trust in Allah puts an end to the fear of death, devastation, poverty and helplessness. It rectifies the biggest weakness of man, which is fear of annihilation or wretched existence.

It was belief in such forces of the world which made the Muslims of the early era of Islam so active, industrious, bold and gallant. Describing them the Qur'an says:

> *"Such people when warned to fear, those who are gathered against them, (the threat of danger) increased their faith and they cried: Allah is sufficient for us! Most excellent is He in whom we trust!".*

Sūrah Āl 'Imrān, 3:172

> *"So they returned with grace and favour from Allah, and no harm touched them. They followed the good pleasure of Allah, and Allah is of infinite bounty".*

Sūrah Āl 'Imrān, 3:173-174

From the foregoing it is clear that there is a vast difference between a belief in fate and destiny based on the Qur'anic teachings and a materialistic belief in it in accordance with the materialistic theory of causation.

All that a materialist believes is that the more efforts he puts to achieve his objective, the better results he is likely to obtain. But a Muslim having faith in destiny believes that the world has been so arranged that the whole system of causes and effects will come to his aid if he whole-heartedly exerts himself to serve the cause of his creed. His power naturally increases thousands of times when the energy stored in the world comes to his aid.

CHAPTER 12

Special Logic of the Holy Qur'an

We previously said that the Muslim theologians started discussing and analyzing the question of human compulsion and liberty in the second half of the first century of the Hijri era. This question is the oldest scholastic problem. Somehow the scholastic theologians could not analyze the question correctly with the result that they deviated from the right path. Some of them supported the theory of predestination and others that of absolute human liberty. To the Muslim masses a belief in destiny meant predestination. They considered belief in human liberty to be tantamount to the negation of destiny. A simultaneous belief in destiny and liberty, though it was acceptable to the clear conscience of the early Muslims, lost its popularity once it took on a philosophical colour. Even now after a lapse of 14 centuries it does not find favour with the Muslim masses, though the Holy Qur'an, the *ḥadīths* of the Holy Prophet and the sayings of the Holy Imams clearly say that everything is governed by the destiny ordained by Allah, and at the same time describe man as an effective factor in making or marring his fortune. They hold him responsible for all his actions. We have in the foregoing quoted some of the Qur'anic verses dealing with these points.

As we have pointed out, the predestinarians have tried to explain away the verses indicating human freedom and the supporters of absolute liberty have tried to explain away the verses indicating that everything is divinely ordained. As we have seen actually there is no inconsistency between these two sets of verses. The riddle stands solved. The comprehensiveness of destiny does not necessarily mean that there is no such thing as destiny. As such the question of any contradiction between destiny and human volition does not arise, and there is no need to explain away anything.

For example the Qur'an says that it is Allah who guides the people to the right or the wrong path, who bestows on them honour, power and health and who provides them with the means of living: Even the virtue and the vice both have been ascribed to His Will.

The Holy Qur'an says:

"It is Allah to leave in error whom He will and to guide whom He pleases. He is the Mighty, the Wise".

Sūrah Ibrāhīm, 14:4

"Say: O Allah! Owner of Sovereignty! You bestow sovereignty on whomever you will and you withdraw sovereignty from whomever you will. You exalt whomever you will and you abase whom you will. In Your hand is all that is good. No doubt you have power to do everything".

Sūrah Āl 'Imrān, 3:26

"Surely Allah is the provider of everything and the possessor of Mighty Power".

Sūrah Al-Dhāriyāt, 51:58

"In the heaven is your providence and that which you are promised".

Sūrah Al-Dhāriyāt, 51:22

The Holy Qur'an quotes Ibrahim as having said:

"He gives me food and drink. If I fall sick, He cures me. He will cause me to die, and will bring me back to life".

Sūrah Al-Shu'arā', 26:79-81

About the happy and the evil things the Qur'an says:

"Say: Everything is from Allah".

Sūrah Al-Nisā', 4:78

But these verses do not deny the intervention of the natural causes. Hence there is no contradiction between them and the other verses which clearly show that it is man himself who chooses the right or the right or the wrong path, acquires power and honour, and earns his livelihood.

For example, the Qur'an says:

"As for Thamud, We showed them the right path, but they preferred blindness to guidance, consequently they were bit by the humiliating punishment of a dreadful noise which they deserved because of their misdeeds".

Sūrah Fuṣṣilat, 41:17

Referring to the downfall of Pharaoh's gang, the Holy Qur'an says:

"That is because Allah does not withdraw the favour He has bestowed on any people unless they first change what is in their hearts, and that is because Allah is Hearer, Knower".

Sūrah al-Anfāl, 8:53

Criticizing the predestinarian belief of the pagan Arabs, the Holy Qur'an says:

"When it is said to them: Give in charity out of what Allah has provided you, the disbelievers say to those who believe: Are we to feed those whom Allah would feed if He willed? Surely you are in a clear error".

Sūrah Yā Sīn, 36:47

Again the Holy Qur'an says:

"Corruption has become rife in land and sea because of the misdeeds of the people".

Sūrah Al-Rūm, 30:41

The fact is, as already pointed out, that Allah's Will, His Knowledge and His Decrees do not nullify the system of causation. Actually this whole infinite system springs from His Will and Knowledge and its effectiveness means the effectiveness of His Will.

On this basis it is wrong to say which act is Allah's and which is not His. Such a division is meaningless. If an act has been ascribed to some other being, it cannot be said that it is not

Allah's. The division of work between the Creator and the created is wrong. Any act of a doer is that of Allah also.

There is a *ḥadīth* in the *Tuhaf-ul-Uqul*, which appears to be a letter written by Imam Hadi the tenth Imam, to some of his supporters in Ahwaz (Iran) on the doctrines of predestination, absolute discretion and justice. In this letter he writes:

> "A person asked Imam Ali whether man has power and ability or he lacks them. If he has the power to do things, then how is it possible to say that there is no power nor help but from Allah?"

From the wording of the *ḥadīth* it appears that the questioner believed that man had the power and ability to do things, Hence he was unable to understand how the question of Allah's Will and Divine Decree could fit in.

In reply the Imam said to him:

> "You asked about ability. Do you have this ability with Allah or without Him!" The questioner was baffled. The Imam said: "If you assert that you and Allah share this ability and power, I would put you to death (because you would be claiming to be a co-partner of Allah). If you say that you have this ability without Allah, again I would put you to death (because you would be presuming that you are independent of Allah. Such a presumptions again infidelity, for independence in any affair means independence in essence)."

> "The questioner said: Then what should I say?"

> The Imam said: "You have ability by the Will of Allah, while He has it independently. If He endows you with it, that is His favour. If He takes it away from you, that means He is testing

you. In any case, you should remember that whatever He bestows on you, He is still its owner. If He enables you to do a thing, that thing is still within His power".

In short, this *ḥadīth* indicates that while an effect is ascribed to its cause, it is attributable to Allah also. When we ascribe an act to its normal and natural doer, we ascribe it to its non-self-existing agent, and when we attribute it to Allah, we ascribe it to its self-existing agent. It is Allah who endows things with the power and quality of producing an effect. It is He who bestows the ownership of anything on anyone. But there is one basic difference between the bestowal of ownership by Allah and the transfer of ownership by a man. After a man has transferred the ownership of a thing, it is no longer his property.

But Allah continues to be the owner of a thing even after He has bestowed it on anyone else. His bestowal is not inconsistent with His continued ownership. It is only a manifestation of His being the owner. Similarly Allah endows things with the quality of producing an effect, and at the same time He is the Master of all effects. There are many other *ḥadīths* which support this view.

CHAPTER 13

High Level of the Logic of Islam

A scholar going deep into the study of the questions concerning monotheism, is filled with wonder when he finds that the special logic adopted in this respect by the Holy Qur'an and next to it by the sayings of the Prophet and the Imams, especially Imam Ali is so different and higher not only from the logic of that time but also from that of the later period when scholastic theology had developed and philosophy was flourishing. What the Qur'an and the *ḥadīth* say about destiny and the freedom or constraint of human will, is an example of that logic.

This in itself proves that the Holy Qur'an has sprung from a source which does not belong to this world and that the Holy Prophet who received the Qur'an looked at the realities from quite a different angle. Similarly the knowledge of the logic of the Qur'an which the Holy Family had was different from what the others had.

Where the ideas were too high to be grasped ordinarily, the other people were bewildered, but the Imams described them very clearly and in a realistic manner. It is not surprising that even the Shi'ah theologians were unable to digest this information properly.

When one looks at the statements and comments of such eminent scholars such a Shaykh Mufid, Sayyid Murtaza, Allamah Hilli, Allamah Majlisi in their books of theology and their commentaries on *ḥadīth*, one notices that they have not been free being influenced by the ideas of the Ash'arites and the Mu'tazilies. Their way of thinking is often close to that of either of them. That is why they have been compelled to explain away many Qur'anic verses and the *ḥadīths*. Anyhow, this shortcoming does not lower the position of these eminent scholars. None else in their position could do better, for the comprehension of the special logic of the Holy Qur'an is confined to the spiritual leaders trained in the school of this Holy Book. Others have been able to enter this circle gradually by going deep into the relevant questions and the constant study of the Qur'an and the sayings of the Prophet and the Imams, especially Imam Ali.

Some of our contemporary scholars have shown sufficient ability to analyze the social questions. But when they take up such problems as that of fate and destiny, they are as much bewildered as the scholastic theologians. For instance, we can mention the name of the Egyptian writer, Ahmad Amin who has written the *Fajr al-Islam*, the *Zuh'l al-Islam*, the *Zuhr al-Islam* and the *Yaum al-Islam*.

Ahmad Amin has to a great extent evinced his ability to discuss and analyze social questions, but as far as the question of fate is concerned, he has proved as helpless as the scholastic theologians. Towards the end of his book, *Fajr al-Islam* he has, in a special chapter, discussed the question of predestination and freedom of will, but on the whole it appears that according to him a belief in destiny means predestinarianism. Hence he is not prepared to believe that the *ḥadīths* regarding destiny are authentic. Similarly he is unable to believe that the *Nahj al-Balaghah* is a collection of the sermons and letter of Imam Ali. Of course, he is not blame, because it is due to his lack of knowledge that he is so skeptic. As a rule it may be said that no scholar, whether a European, an Egyptian or an Iranian, whose knowledge is confined to social sciences, is in a position to express an opinion on the history of Islamic knowledge.

Whenever the European historians or the orientalists have expressed an opinion about the question of fate, they have either described Islam as a religion of predestination or have claimed that the doctrine of fate and destiny is not found in the Qur'an and that it was created later by the scholastic theologians.

An orientalist says:

"The cardinal principles of Islam are as follows: God is One: Muḥammad is His Prophet ... The theologians have preached that Allah has foreordained the fate of everybody and that His Will is unchangeable. This doctrine is called *jabr* (pre-destination; literally compulsion) ..."

Gustav Le Bon, in a defending way says that in this respect the Qur'an has not said anything more than what the other sacred Books say. After quoting verses of the Qur'an and making certain remarks he adds,

"Islam has been accused of having a belief in fate, but this charge is as baseless as all other charges. We have already put the Qur'anic verses on this subject before our readers. They say no more than what is written in this respect in our sacred Book. All philosophers and schoolmen are of the view that all events are preordained and totally unchangeable. Luther, who was a reformer, himself has written: "All available evidence in the sacred Book is repugnant to the theory of liberty. This evidence is found in many places of the Scripture. It may be said that all sacred Books are full of such indications".

After referring to the belief in destiny as prevalent among the ancient Greeks and the Romans, he says

"It is clear that Islam has not given more importance to this question than other religions. Islam has not given to it even as much heed as some of the contemporary scholars".

Gustav Le Bon admits that a belief in fate amounts to a belief in predestination and a refutation of freedom of will. But he says that such a belief is found in all religions and most of the philosophical systems.

In his *History of Civilization*, after giving a gist of the Qur'anic verses on the comprehensiveness of Divine Knowledge and Will and referring to a well-known *ḥadīth* found in al-Bukhari's *al-Ṣaḥīḥ*, Will Durant says that "Belief in predestination is a part of the Islamic way of thinking".

Now let us see what Mr. Dominic Sordell has designed to say in this respect. He has written a book, named "Islam". In it he says:

"From the very beginning of the Islamic era the Muslims were conscious of the contradictions in the Qur'an. According to an available report they even pointed out some contradictions to the Prophet himself who in reply said: "Keep believing in what is worrying you". Later the Muslims who did not like to accept certain doctrines off-hand, tried to interpret certain words and expressions of the Qur'an. That is how the science of exegesis developed. The first question which attracted the attention of the Muslims was—If man cannot act contrary to what Allah has preordained and still Allah requites him for his good or bad deeds, does that not constitute a contradiction between Allah's Power and human responsibility? The Qur'an does not answer this question, but the Omnipotence of Allah has been so much emphasized throughout the Qur'an, that no room has been left for human liberty. Thus submission to the Will of Allah prevails over a sense of human responsibility".

Mr. Dominic Sordell's book is full of such kind of research.

This is the way of thinking of the orientalists and that is how they derive their conclusions. This instance shows how far they are able to express an opinion in regard to such a question.

It is clear from the foregoing that the question of fate and destiny has been repeatedly mentioned by the Qur'an itself. It is not an invention of the scholastic theologians. Further, it is also clear that a belief in destiny as taught by the Qur'an is poles apart from predestinarianism.

The European orientalists usually extoll the Mu'tazilite for denying destiny. According to the Mu'tazilites a belief in destiny amounts to a belief in predestination.

There is no doubt if we compare the Mu'tazilites and the Ash'arites, we find that the former had considerable independence of thought. Mutawakkil's suppression of the Mu'tazilites and his official support of the Ash'arites may be regarded as a big tragedy of the world of Islam. But as far as the question of fate and destiny is concerned, the mistake made by the Mu'tazilites was not less grave than that made by the Ash'arites. The orientalists who do not have any deep knowledge of Islam and who are under the impression that a belief in destiny amounts to a belief in predestination are never tired of praying tributes to the Mu'tazilites.

Edward Brown in his *Literary History of Persia* says:

"The Qadarites or the Mu'tazilites were more important. They
advocated freedom of will or absolute discretion. The best
homage which can be paid to the Mu'tazilites is that their
ideas were a protest which common sense always makes
against unjust orders and rigid teachings. The monotheism".

They said that the Ash'arite belief in the eternal fate meant that
Allah had pre-ordained the destiny of everyone, that He punished
the people for the sins which He Himself had imposed on them,
and that man could not resist his destiny.

This way of thinking of the Mu'tazilites, namely that destiny
meant predestination, has received the highest approbation of the
orientalists.

Historical Background

The origin of the controversy regarding fate is a point worth
discussion. The point is how it was that from the first half or at the
most from the second half of the first century the Muslims entered
into the discussion of predestination and free will.

Undoubtedly the reason was that the Qur'anic verses and the
Prophetic sayings referred to this question. It is a question which
naturally attracts the attention of everybody. As it was raised in the
Holy Book and as some of the verses expressly supported destiny
while some others described man as having liberty, naturally the
Muslims had to think over this question and discuss it.

But the orientalists and their lackeys claim that these ideas
have some other basis.

As we have already said, some European historians believe
that the question of destiny was raised later by the scholastic
theologians. Originally Islam preached neither predestination nor

free will. Some other orientalists are of the view that the Ash'arite theory based on predestination represents the true teaching of Islam, but the Mu'tazilites did not acquiesce in it as they did not accept many other Islamic ideas which were not in conformity with logic and reason. It were they who for the first time introduced the idea of free will among the Muslims. These orientalists further say that even the Mu'tazilites were not the originators of this idea. They were influenced by the neighbouring nations, especially the Christians.

Edward Brown in the '*Literary History of Persia*' says: Von Cromer is of the view that Ma'bad al-Juhani preached the idea of free will in Damascus towards the end of the 7th century is imitation of an Iranian named Sanbawayh.

He further says:

"According to Von Cromer, Damascus was the place where the doctrines of the Mu'tazilites developed under the influence of the Byzantine Christian divines, especially John of Damascus and his disciple, Theodorus Abu Kurra".

It appears that in the opinion of Von Cromer even that Iranian who suggested the idea of freedom and liberty of Ma'bad al-Juhani, was himself influenced by the Roman-Christian ecclesiastics.

If this view is accepted, we will have to look for a similar historical basis for prayer, fasting monotheism and the belief in the hereafter. Probably the Muslims paid attention to these also because they had found a precedent for them in the Christian circles.

The fact is that the orientalists do not possess enough

competence to make an inquiry into the Islamic tenets, nor mostly do they have good intention.

When they try to analyze Islamic concepts or deal with Islamic tenets, mysticism or Muslim philosophy, they put forth such astonishingly absurd ideas that they are often ridiculous. For instance look at the following remarks of an orientalist.

Edward Brown in his Literary *History of Persia, vol. 1*, quotes the Dutch orientalist as saying in his *History of Islam*:

> "When they (the Mu'tazilites) gave serious thought to the rules of Islam, they advocated only what was reasonable. Thus one of the points which they emphasized was that Qur'an was transient and created, though to say so was against what the Prophet (ṣ) had declared. They said that the eternity of the Qur'an meant a belief in the eternity of two beings, while the correct position was that the Qur'an, which was the word of Allah was His creation. Further, it could not be attributed to His essence, for that was unchangeable.

> Thus the basis of revelation was shaken. Many Mu'tazilites openly said that it was not impossible to produce a writing like the Qur'an or even better than that.

> This orientalist wants to impress on us implicitly that the Ash'arites had derived their belief in the eternity of the Qur'an from the sayings of the Prophet (ṣ) and that though the Mu'tazilite knew that, they rejected this doctrine because they found it contrary to the dictates of reason and logic. In this very book he says a little further that the eternity of the Qur'an was one of the doctrines of the Ash'arites who faithfully follow the text of the Qur'an.

> In fact in the Qur'an there is not even a slightest hint to the

eternity of the Qur'an or to its being uncreated, nor there exists to this effect a single *ḥadīth* acceptable to the Mu'tazilites.

That is why they opposed the idea that the Qur'an was a Celestial Book and that it was revealed.[5]

Their belief about Allah was purer and more sublime, than that held by the pietists, the adherents to the popular notions and the Ash'arites. The Mu'tazilites never accepted the idea that the Creator of the world could ever appear in a corporeal form. They were not willing to listen to such a thing. There is a *ḥadīth*, according to which the Prophet said: "Just as you saw the full moon during the Battle of Badr, one day you will see Allah also."[6]

He means a report, which is found in the books of scholastic theology and not those of *ḥadīth*. According to this report the Holy Prophet (ṣ) said:

"You will see your Lord on the Day of Resurrection as you see the full moon". The learned orientalist mistook in the report

---

[5] There is enough historical evidence to show that the Mu'tazilites were the staunch supporters and defenders of the Qur'an. They fought relentlessly against the heresies of the Zindiqs (atheists) and the philosophers. If as Dozy claims, they did not regard the Qur'an as revealed, why did they take the trouble of defending it?

[6] It is an unforgivable mistake of the Ash'arites to believe that human eye will see Allah on the Day of Resurrection. Such an idea is contrary to what the Qur'an has expressly said. *"No eyes can see Him, but He comprehends all vision. He is the Subtle, all Aware"*. (Sūrah Al-Anʿām, 6:103)Anyhow, there is a truth which has been described as "meeting Allah". But there are many *ḥadīths* which confirm that this is not a corporeal matter. (For details please see, Murtaza Mutahhari, *Master and Mastership*, ISP, 1980).

the word, *badr* meaning the full moon for the Battle of Badr. Then he translated the future tense into the past so that the sentence might give some meaning.

This report has a long story. There are indications that it was once deformed by someone among its transmitters. Then it was again distorted by the scholastic theologians. It is for the third time that the learned orientalist has put it in a ludicrous form. The Qur'an expressly denies the possibility that a human eye can see Allah.

As the pietists took this *ḥadīth* literally, the Mu'tazilites found it to be a big hurdle in their way and were compelled to explain it away. They said that man after death would see Allah with spiritual eyes. The Mu'tazilites also denied that Allah was the Creator of the infidels.[7]

This is an example of the valuable research of a learned orientalist. Edward Brown; the author of the 'Literary History of Persia' passed it over without making any comments.

We wonder whether we should call it ignorance or a crime. What is more regrettable is that the followers and lackeys of these orientalists, instead of studying the ideas of the East and the Islamic tenets directly, continue to repeat the views of their master parrot-like.

---

[7] In history there has not been a single Mu'tazilite who ever said that Allah was not the Creator of the infidels. All that the Mu'tazilites said was that Allah was not the Creator of infidelity, injustice and sin. They never said that He was not the Creator of the infidels, the unjust and the sinners.

CHAPTER 14

Some *Ḥadīths* to the Contrary

There are some *ḥadīths* which appear to be contrary to what we have said. But their contradiction is either superficial or due to the fact that owing to some misunderstanding they were misquoted by one of their transmitters. In the first case the contradiction disappears when we go deep into the reports and in the second case the mistake can be rectified by comparing the *ḥadīths* in question with other reports on the subject. We give below an example of each type. Let us take the second case first.

A *ḥadīth* has been mentioned in al-Bukhari's *al-Ṣaḥīḥ* on the authority of Yahya bin Yamar, according to which ʿĀʾishah, Mother of the Faithful, says that she asked the Holy Prophet about the epidemic of plague.

> He said: "It was a scourge sent by Allah unto whom He willed. Now it has been made a blessing for the Muslims. A person who stays in the affected town, shows patience and believes that nothing will befall him except what Allah has ordained, will receive the same reward as a martyr".

Now we quote another *ḥadīth* on this very subject. It is mentioned in *al-Kafi*, vol. VIII. According to it Ubaydullah al-Halabi asked Imam Ja'far al-Sadiq whether a person was allowed to move out of a place where plague had broken out?

> The Imam said: "There is no harm. The Prophet only forbade the leaving of a place which was situated in front of the enemy position. When plague broke out there and the people began to flee from it, the Prophet said that he who fled from there, would be considered to have run away from a battlefield. The Prophet said so because he did not want the Muslims to desert their position.

It is clear from the explanation given by Imam Sadiq that the reason why the Holy Prophet forbade fleeing from plague on a particular occasion was that he wanted to impress upon the Muslims that they must stick to their duty and must not expose themselves to a bigger risk. He did not issue a general instruction that the Muslims should not take precautionary measures against plague and should sit simply awaiting what was in store for them. A Muslim is duty bound to protect his life and property.

As the saying of the Holy Prophet passed through a number of transmitters, it took the shape of a general rule as we find it in its present form in al-Bukhari. Fortunately the real intention of the Holy Prophet has been disclosed by Imam Sadiq, who naturally knew it better than anybody else, for he himself was a member of *Ahl al-Bayt al-Rasul* (the Holy Family).

It is also possible that the *ḥadīth* of al-Bukhari may have some other background and intention. The Holy Prophet might have asked the people not to move out of a plague ridden town so that they might not transmit the epidemic to other places. In olden days there existed no means of treating this disease, nor there were any quarantine arrangements. The only possible precaution against the spreading of the disease was that the people should not move out of the infected place.

Recounting Umar's Journey to Syria, Ibn Abi al-Hadid in his commentary on the *Nahj al-Balaghah*, Sermon 132 says: "

> On hearing that plague was raging in a particular town of Syria, Umar decided not to visit that place. In reply to Abu Ubaydah ibn al-Jarrah, who had objected to his fleeing from a divinely ordained destiny, he said that Abd Al-Rahman ibn Awf had told him that the Holy Prophet had said; "If plague breaks out in a place, do not enter it, if you are not already inside it, but if you are, do not leave it".

Either, the *ḥadīth* of *Ṣaḥīḥ al-Bukhari* is related to that incident which has been explained by Imam Sadiq or it is an instruction to the effect that the people of an infected area should not go to any other place. In either case it is certain that its significance is not what it apparently indicates, and that its transmitters have misunderstood it.

There is another report in *al-Kafi*, vol. II. According to it Imam Sadiq is reported to have said:

> "One day Imam Ali was sitting with some people under a dilapidated wall. Someone asked him not to sit under that wall because it was tottering. The Commander of the Faithful said that one's appointed time (time appointed for his death) guards him. No sooner he left the place than the wall fell down".

Imam Sadiq added that the Commander of the Faithful used

to do such things often. That is what is called *Yaqeen* (Conviction).

It may be said that this *ḥadīth* is not in keeping with what we mentioned earlier and according to which Asbagh bin Nubatah reported that Imam Ali moved away from the bent wall and on being criticized for fleeing from one divinely ordained destiny, he said that he was fleeing from one divinely ordained destiny to another. How is it that when Ali, himself moves away from a bent wall and he is criticized for doing that, he says that he was fleeing from destiny to another and when he is asked by someone else to do that, he says that the 'appointed time' guards him?

Further, according to the Islamic law it is not permissible to sit under a tottering wall. Then how is it that Imam Ali did not leave the place under the plea that he was guarded by his 'appointed time'?

It appears that keeping in view what we have said earlier, this *ḥadīth* can be interpreted in a way that it would neither be inconsistent with the *ḥadīth* of Asbagh bin Nubatah nor with the legal principle enjoining the protection of one's own life.

While discussing the spiritual factor we said that the sequence of the causes affecting a destiny could not be confined to the three dimension material causes of this world. The spiritual causes are also equally effective. Sometimes it so happens that when we look at an event from its material angle only, it appears that the sequence of its causes is complete, but if we look at it from another angle and observe some secret aspects of it, we realize that some spiritual causes to the contrary and other good deeds performed with good intention make an impact on the system of causation. If somebody has a sense additional to those senses which we all normally have, his judgement in certain cases may be quite different from that of ours. This case may be illustrated by an example.

We are three-dimensional beings. Our judgements about three-dimensional matters will naturally be different from that of two-dimensions. But as far as two dimensional matters are considered, our judgement and their judgement will be the same. The people who are endowed with 'conviction' have an additional sense and they look at things from a different angle. Naturally on certain occasions their judgement is different from ours.

We may regard a thing as a cause of death, but a man of conviction may not think so, because he has an eye on certain inner force at work. From spiritual point of view there is no reason why we should not believe that certain things are spiritually effective in causing prolongation of life, maintenance of health and expansion of the means of living, and that the people endowed with conviction are aware of them.

Anyway, this *hadīth* can be explained, though it requires a lengthy explanation.

CHAPTER 15

Could Allah's Knowledge be Wrong?

At the end of this discussion of fate and destiny it will not be out of place to take up the criticism made in this connection by the predestinarians and to analyze what they say They have adduced many and varied arguments to prove their theory. The Muslim predestinarians mainly rely on the Qur'anic verses regarding fate which we have already quoted. Sometimes they cite the sayings of the Holy Prophet or the Imams in this connection.

We have commented upon the intellectual arguments advanced by them in the footnotes of our book, *The Principles of Philosophy,* vol. III.

The most famous argument which they have advanced concerns the Knowledge of Allah. They say that Allah knows from eternity what will happen. No event is hidden from His Eternal Knowledge.

At the same time His Knowledge is unchangeable. Any change in it will not be in keeping with His perfectness. It is not possible that anything should happen contrary to what He knows from eternity Otherwise His Knowledge will prove to be defective, and instead of being knowledge, it will become ignorance, which is again against the perfectness of His Being.

Hence on the basis of the two premises that: Allah knows everything; and His Divine Knowledge is unchangeable and nothing can happen contrary to it, it may be inferred logically, that every event in the world must take place in accordance with what He knows from eternity.

Furthermore, Divine Knowledge is active and not passive, in the sense that in the case of Allah the known springs from His Knowledge of it, and His Knowledge is not based on the known as is the case with human knowledge of the things and the events.

On this basis of Allah knew that such and such person at such and such time would commit a sin, he is bound to commit it accordingly. It will not be possible for him to behave otherwise. No power on earth can stop him from committing that sin at the appointed time. Otherwise Allah's Knowledge will prove wrong.

The world famous Persian poet Umar Khayyam says:

> I drink wine; and a sound person
> Should have no objection to that;
> God knew from eternity that I would;
> If I don't, His knowledge would amount to ignorance.

For a man who is aware of the correct conception of fate and destiny it is easy to refute this specious argument, based on the presumption that Divine Knowledge in eternity was attached to the occurrences haphazardly; and now to ensure that the prior Divine Knowledge should not go wrong and everything should occur according to the prearranged plan, it is necessary that all events should be controlled.

To advance this argument it has been presumed that Divine Knowledge attaches to the occurrence and the non-occurrence of events independently of the system of causation, and that it is imperative to control this system and, where necessary, to curb the natural laws and the liberty of human will in order t ensure that there should be no inconsistency between the Divine Eternal Knowledge and what actually happens.

On the basis of this conception it is necessary to deprive man of his power, liberty and will so that his actions may be brought under control.

But this conception of Divine Knowledge itself is totally wrong and based on complete ignorance. It is impossible that Allah's Knowledge should attach to the occurrence or the non-occurrence of an event haphazardly and then it should be necessary to bring about any change in the firm and stable system of causation or to curb a natural law or the liberty of human will.

In this circumstance it appears to be very unlikely that the above quoted lines should be genuinely of Khayyam who was at least a semi-philosopher. Perhaps they have been wrongly ascribed to him after his death. Anyhow, if they are really his, then it may be said that he has only versified an idea in a beautiful style, but these verses do not represent his philosophy. Khayyam is known all over the world for his striking ideas and beautiful style.

The Eternal Knowledge of Allah cannot be detached from the system of causation. His Knowledge is actually the knowledge of that system, and it makes it necessary that this world should exist with its specific systems. It does not attach to the occurrence or the nonoccurrence of an event direct and irrespective of its causes. The Divine Knowledge in fact attaches to the emanation of an event from its particular cause and agent. The causes and agents are varied. Some causes are natural, while some others are conscious. Similarly some agents are free, having the power of choosing, whereas some others are not. What the Knowledge of Allah necessitates is that due effect should be produced by its due agent. It does not render it possible that the effect of a free agent should emanate from an agent not actually free.

In other words the Eternal Knowledge of Allah is the knowledge of a system. Allah knows that such and such effect will be produced by such and such cause. But all causes and the agents are not alike. Some causes are conscious and some others are not. Some agents are free and some others are not. Allah knows them as they are. It would be even better to say that they are as Allah knows them. What the Divine Knowledge requires is that the act of a free agent should emanate from a free agent and the act of a non-free agent should emanate from a non-free agent.

As we have stated earlier, man in this world has a particular sort of freedom and choice. As far as his acts are concerned, he has such potentialities as other things in existence including animals, do not have divine knowledge being the source of everything in existence, the whole system as it actually exists is based on what is known to Allah. His Eternal Knowledge attaches to human acts and deeds in the sense that He knows from eternity who will do his duty of his own will and who will commit sins of his own will. Allah's Knowledge requires that he who obeys Him does so of his own will and he who disobeys Him also does so of his own will. That is why it is said that man is free performance. He cannot help being at liberty. The Eternal Knowledge of Allah does not force anyone to commit a sin nor does it deprive anyone of his liberty as already determined by His Knowledge.

Hence both the premises mentioned above on which the

criticism was based are false and do not hold good. It is true that Divine Knowledge is active and not passive. But that does not mean that man has no choice. When he commits a sin he is not compelled by an external force. He has been created free and Allah knows that when man does a thing he does it of his own free will. If he were forced to do a thing that would have meant that Allah's Knowledge is wrong. The critic who says that Allah knew from eternity that he would drink wine, should be asked to explain whether Allah knew that he would drink it of his own will or He knew that he would be compelled by an external force to do so. Evidently what Allah knew from eternity was neither forced drinking, nor drinking simply. It was voluntary drinking that He knew. Hence Divine Knowledge would prove wrong if he drank by compulsion. The Divine Knowledge of the acts and deeds of the beings having freedom of will does not mean compulsion at all. It means just the opposite. Men must enjoy the freedom of will with which they have been endowed. He was right who said that it is height of ignorance to regard Divine Knowledge as the cause of sinning.

All this was about Divine Knowledge from the angle of its being eternal and prior to every happening. It is this aspect of Divine Knowledge which the Qur'an has called the Book, the *Protected Tablet, the Pen, etc.*

Anyhow it should be remember that while all things in this world and its entire system of causation are known to Allah, they at the same time constitute His Knowledge also. This world and all its systems are Allah's Knowledge as well as known to Him. Nothing can be hidden from Him. He is everywhere and with everything.

The Holy Qur'an says:

"Wherever you turn, you are always in the presence of Allah".

Sūrah Al-Baqarah, 2:115

Allah in the Holy Qur'an says:

"We are nearer to him than his jugular vein".

Sūrah Qāf, 50:16

"He is the First and the Last, and the Manifest and the Unseen; and He knows all things".

Sūrah Al-Ḥadīd, 57:3

Thus the whole world with all its characteristics and systems is an aspect of Allah's Knowledge.

At this stage of knowledge, the known and the knowledge are identical. They are one and not two. Therefore the question of consistency or inconsistency between them, does not arise. It cannot be said that in such and such case Allah's Knowledge will be right and that otherwise it will be wrong.

References

Source URL: https://www.al-islam.org/man-and-his-destiny-ayat
ullah-murtadha-mutahhari

Links

1. https://www.al-islam.org/user/login?destination=node/13088
   %23comment-form

2. https://www.al-islam.org/user/register?destination=node/130
   88%23comment-form

3. https://www.al-islam.org/person/ayatullah-murtadha-mutahh
   ari

4. https://www.al-islam.org/organization/islamic-seminary-pub
   lications

5. https://www.al-islam.org/library/philosophy

6. https://www.al-islam.org/tags/destiny

7. https://www.al-islam.org/tags/free-will

8. https://www.al-islam.org/tags/gods-knowledge

9. https://www.al-islam.org/tags/divine-decree

10. https://www.al-islam.org/person/ahlul-bayt

Index

www.ingramcontent.com/pod-product-compliance
Lightning Source LLC
Chambersburg PA
CBHW032008040426
42448CB00006B/541